"There is no greater agony than bearing an untold story inside you." ~Maya Angelou

BY THE SAME AUTHOR

The Light
A Novel

Finding the Light Within
A Spiritual Guide to True Peace,
Happiness, Freedom and Enlightenment

Ready When You Are
Cecil B. DeMille's Ten Commandments for Success

C. B. DeMille
The Man Who Invented Hollywood

Blockbuster Resumes
Insider's Secrets to Dazzle Your Audience
and Blow Away the Competition

Identity Theft
How to Protect Your Most Valuable Asset

Life After Debt
Free Yourself from the Burden of Money
Worries Once and for All

Credit Secrets
How to Erase Bad Credit

TRANSFORMED BY WRITING

How to Change Your Life and Change the World with the Power of Story

Robert Hammond

Library of Congress Control Number: 2013916742

ISBN-13: 978-0615875958
ISBN-10: 0615875955

Transformed by Writing:
How to Change Your Life and Change the World
with the Power of Story
New Way Press
www.newwaypress.com

Walnut Creek, CA 94597

Cover design by Dumitru Radu.

Acknowledgements

Thank you to everyone who helped transform this book from concept to print and beyond. Utmost thanks goes to my wife Lesa Hammond who encouraged and supported me during the process and was instrumental in the editing, formatting, and publication. Thanks always to my mother, father, and son who have always been supportive, loving, and encouraging in every way. To Fay Guilian and Laura Danielle for your input and encouragement during the editing of this book.

To Christine Kloser, the transformational catalyst who heralded my call to adventure. To Philippe "SHOCK" Matthews, the "Oprah of the internet," for airing the revealing interview about my life, which became the final section of this book titled, *Good Friday: A Writer's Journey from Prison to Pardon*. To producer Dan Sagrue and host Nick Digilio at WGN radio in Chicago for the interview that was transcribed into the chapter, *The Return: A Writer Gives Back.*

To Terri Zinner at A Film Writer for inviting me to participate in the teleseminar on adapting your book to screen. To Paul Klein and his wonderful and efficient staff at Internet

Transcribers for transforming my teleseminars, interviews, and video classes into the written word.

To Nat Mundel and the dynamic staff at Voyage Media for providing me with feedback, support, development help, and the latest trends on adapting my own and many other books to the big screen. To Meredith Watkins and Josie Ramirez-Herndon at Recovery View for bringing my work to the attention of the substance abuse treatment professionals community around the world.

To Frank Montesonti, Colin Dickey, Ariane Simard, Helen Kantor, and the other faculty and advisors at National University Creative Writing Program, who helped transform my storytelling skills to a new level.

Other allies and mentors—including some of whom I have never met—who helped along my storytelling journey through words of wisdom, encouragement, inspiration, and in many other ways include: Maya Angelou, Jane Dystel, Bruce Joel Rubin, Tim Ferris, Derek Rydall, Chris Vogler, Steve Harrison, Jack Canfield, Anne Lamott, Peter Anthony Holder, Chuck Gallagher, Rhonda Gould Smolarek, Professor Ronald L Mallett, William Timmons, Brian Floyd, Gabrielle Evans-Fields, Julia Cameron, Amanda Gillespie, Susan Straight, Robert McKee, Joe Vitale, SARK, Fabienne Fredrickson, Sandy Powell, Wendy Keller, Linda

Joy, Ellen Violette, Bill Gladstone, Linda Siversten, Reid Tracy, Nancy Jeutten, Gail Larsen, Christina Hills, Kate Buck, Lisa Nichols, Susan Harrow, Sharla Jacobs, Amy Ahlers, Noah St. John, Marianne Williamson, and Hall V. Worthington.

Table of Contents

Why this Book?

When a mentally ill gunman stormed a suburban Atlanta elementary school with an AK-47 and started shooting, bookkeeper Antoinette Tuff calmed him down by sharing tragic stories from her own life. The gunman surrendered to authorities and nobody was injured. Sharing her story saved the lives of countless children and school employees. Her story changed lives.

As a creative writing professor, author of over a dozen books and writer of several scripts that have made it to the screen, I have long been aware of the power of story. Over the years I have witnessed many people change their lives and inspire change in the lives of others through the sharing of stories. Along the way I've helped many people bring their stories to light through book and screen and other venues. Others just want to leave a legacy for their friends and family. My personal journey of healing, transformation, and recovery was facilitated through telling my own story and from hearing the life-changing stories of others.

After the recent publication of my novel, *The Light,* I planned to take a break from writing for a while. Having already retired from my previous career with the government, I was busy enough teaching a couple of college classes and doing a little creative consulting on the side. Little did I know that when writing coach Christine Kloser invited me to her *Transformational Author Experience,* everything was about to change. During that same time I also completed a program on book to screen adaptation with Nat Mundel and his team at Voyage Media. Soon afterwards, I was asked to write an article on *Creative Writing and Recovery* for the *Recovery View* publication for substance abuse treatment professionals. Several radio interviews shortly followed where I had a chance to reveal some personal details about my life and the transformational process of storytelling. Three months later the book you are now reading was finished.

Transformed by Writing combines time-tested ancient wisdom with personal experience, extensive research and the latest media trends to provide you with a comprehensive experience for helping you become a published author or produced screenwriter and shine your light in the world. This book was developed from original, previously unpublished material, including many hours of transcribed interviews, teleseminars, classroom videos, along with articles and special reports related to creative writing, personal transformation, recovery, spirituality, publishing, screenwriting, and adaptation to film and television.

Feel free to read this book any way you like – from front to back, or back to front or starting in the middle. You may just pick a random page or section and start reading as you are led. If you want to start with the last page and read my bio first, then move through the press releases before you come back to the beginning, that is perfectly fine as well. I would, however, encourage you to read the book in its entirety and go back through it again to focus on the areas that most strongly draw your attention. I've purposely left the interviews, classes, and teleseminars as close as possible to their original formats in order to provide you with the experience of being in the classroom or on the phone with me. I also found that much easier than editing everything to make it seems like I had just written this book from scratch.

The purpose of this book is to provide you with practical tools and personal insights to help you along your journey to share your story with the world. On a practical level, you will learn how to prepare, organize, write, publish, promote, and adapt your story to film or television. On a professional level, you will be transformed from being a writer to becoming a published author, produced screenwriter or leading expert in your field. On another level your life will be transformed as you impact the lives of others with the power of story. Ultimately, your transformation will play an essential part in changing the world.

The question to you now is why do you want to write your book? Are you ready to tell your story so you can begin to change your life and change the world? Adventure calls.

Ready when you are,

What if…?

What if you woke up blindfolded and tied to a chair? A distant voice asks, "Where is it?"

We'll come back to that scene later. Meanwhile, let's look at a more personal and realistic question.

What if you went through life without ever trying to get your book published or telling your story to the world? What would be your BIGGEST regret?

Here are the five most common deathbed regrets of aspiring authors:

- I'd never know if I could have made it.
- I'd never find my voice.
- I'd never get to show others what I'm capable of doing.
- I'd hate not having the freedom to do what I want.

And the number one regret is:

- I couldn't live a life true to myself.

Nobody wants to come to the end of their life filled with deep regrets. And you don't have to … if you take the right actions now.

Begin by asking yourself the following questions:

1. Will I regret never knowing if I could have succeeded as an author?
2. Could my words make a difference in someone else's life?
3. Do I want people to know who I really am?
4. Do I want to pursue my vision now instead of waiting until it's too late?
5. Do I have a story that needs to be told?

If you answered "yes" to any of these questions, you're not alone. You're in the right place right now. Welcome home.

A Distant Memory

I entered the department store and tried my best to look halfway like a real shopper. Something told me they were watching me. Maybe it was just my drug-induced paranoia, I told myself, half-convincingly. I picked up a pair of slacks, folding them over my arm neatly. I turned and headed down another aisle, this time deftly slipping a belt and a handful of silk ties beneath the pants. I then headed to the dressing room to do my dirty work. I entered an empty stall and wrapped the belt and ties around my waist, covering them with my shirt. I tucked the shirt in carefully and straightened out my jacket, making sure nothing was bulging or hanging out. Then I exited the dressing room and put the pants back on the rack where I had found them.

They're watching you. Eyes piercing your soul. You're naked for everybody to see. Don't you know that everyone is watching you now? You can't hide anymore. They all know. They all see you. They hear your thoughts. The sound of your pounding heart echoes over the loud speakers as all of the store employees and all of the customers stop and listen. They turn toward you and watch you with accusing eyes. Penetrating eastern eyes burn with laser-light intensity through your naked soul. No place to run. No place to hide. It's over now. They know what you've done. They know who you really are. They all see you. You're naked.

I was in a movie watching myself play out that final scene. But I couldn't change the script. I was trapped in this moment of destiny. I watched from the audience as two security guards tackled me just outside the front door. Like a video recorder, the action stopped and then replayed itself in slow motion. I watched as they cuffed my hands behind my back and dragged me into the security office. I saw the police officers come in and place me under arrest and haul me down to the station.

The next thing I remember was looking up at the ceiling. A white light glared down at me. The room was white. A man in white looked down at me and laughed. He put his face close to mine and stared into my eyes mockingly. He turned to his assistant and said, "Hey, you want to see what a black guy with jaundice looks like?" I couldn't see who he was talking to at first, but I knew that someone else was in the room. I whispered, "What's going to happen?"

"Looks like you'll probably be dead by

Christmas" the man in white jeered. His laughter faded into sterile walls as the words echoed in my brain, "DEAD BY CHRISTMAS"... "DEAD BY CHRISTMAS"... "DEAD BY CHRISTMAS." This was Thanksgiving. I closed my eyes as I slipped in and out of consciousness.

You're going to die and it matters to no one, least of all to you. At least the pain of this life would end and you will cease to destroy the lives of all those whose paths you've crossed. You think back over the years of running through people's lives like a wild hurricane, leaving behind only shattered glass and splinters. There is nobody left to turn to. The world will be a better place without you as your life now comes to its vile and well deserved finality: To die. In jail. Alone.

The Three Assassins stand by your bedside. Fear, Guilt and Resentment taunt you with every sin you have ever committed.

They shout their filthy curses and accusations at you until you cover your ears with your hands and beg them to stop.

And they don't stop.

You know you have to end it all. You are beyond hope, beyond salvation. Your grace period has run out.

I wrap the bed sheet around my neck and tie it into a hangman's noose, fastening the end to the top of the bars. I leap into the Abyss.

The Power of Story

Imagine an ancient storyteller sitting behind a huge fire as sparks fly up into the dark sky. His eyes glisten with tears in the firelight as diamonds lace the velvet night. He points to the ragged scar on the side of his face and describes his fierce battle with the leopard that ripped his younger brother to shreds.

From the beginning of civilization, storytellers have transmitted wisdom, carried forward traditions, and revealed the secrets of the universe. Stories connect us on a cellular and neurochemical level. Our brains need stories for survival. When we hear and connect with a story, we put ourselves in the shoes of the hero and learn the lessons of survival, hope, and triumph as well as those of loss and grief and tragedy.

Many years ago, a lady worked as a transfusion volunteer at Stanford Hospital. She became acquainted with a little girl named Liza who was suffering from a rare disease and needed a blood transfusion. The little girl had a five-year-old brother who was a perfect candidate for the procedure, for he had miraculously survived the same disease and had developed the antibodies needed to combat the life threatening illness.

The doctor explained the situation to her parents and asked the boy if he would be willing to give his blood to his sister. The boy hesitated and asked if he could think about it overnight. The next morning he approached his parents and hesitated for a moment before taking a deep breath and saying, "Yes, I'll do it if it will save Liza."

As the transfusion progressed, the boy lay in bed next to his sister and smiled. Everyone was happy to see the color returning to the little girl's cheeks, but soon the boy's face grew pale and his smile faded. He looked up at the doctor and asked, "When will I start to die?"

Stories are powerful. Stories change lives. Whether the above story actually happened exactly as described or not, the point of self-sacrifice and courage was made in a moving and dramatic way. The story will be remembered more than if someone had simply preached a sermon on the importance of helping others.

Here is one of the shortest stories ever told: For sale: Baby shoes, never worn. How would you write your story in only six words? Mine might go something like, Transformed by writing: Into the Light. What's your story?

The Parable of the Sower

Again, Jesus began to teach by the lake. The crowd that gathered around him was so large that he got into a boat and sat in it out on the lake, while all the people were along the shore at the water's edge. He taught them many things by parables, and in his teaching said: "Listen! A farmer went out to sow his seed. As he was scattering the seed, some fell along the path, and the birds came and ate it up. Some fell on rocky places, where it did not have much soil. It sprang up quickly, because the soil was shallow. But when the sun came up, the plants were scorched, and they withered because they had no root. Other seed fell among thorns, which grew up and choked the plants, so that they did not bear grain. Still other seed fell on good soil. It came up, grew and produced a crop, some multiplying thirty, some sixty, some a hundred times."

Then Jesus said, "Whoever has ears to hear, let them hear."

When he was alone, the Twelve and the others around him asked him about the parables. He told them, "The secret of the kingdom of God has been given to you. But to those on the outside everything is said in parables so that, "'they may be ever seeing but never perceiving, and ever hearing but never understanding; otherwise they might turn and be forgiven!'"

Then Jesus said to them, "Don't you understand this parable? How then will you understand any parable?"

Jesus spoke all these things to the crowd in parables; he did not say anything to them without using a parable. So was fulfilled what was spoken through the prophet:

"I will open my mouth in parables, I will utter things hidden since the creation of the world."

What does that all mean to you? Things are not always as they seem. Have you ever heard a story and then later realized that it contained some profound lesson?

A parable is a story with a deeper, hidden meaning; a secret, inner story within an outer story. The meaning is often directed to a certain audience while being deliberately hidden from others. What are some of these secret stories that have transformed your life on the deepest levels? What is your own deep story? How could your story transform the lives of others? How could you transform the world? What if…?

May the eyes of your understanding be enlightened.

Transform Your Writing – Transform Your Life

What's your story?

Can you imagine writing a book or making a movie that changes lives or changes the world? What if you could take your writing to another level? Do you have a story that you'd love to see adapted to the big screen or a television series? Do you have a message or some expertise that you've wanted to share with the world? You're not alone.

You are now standing at the threshold of an opportunity so profound and so far-reaching that it is almost impossible to imagine.

What if you could transform your life by the time it takes to finish reading this book? Are you ready to take your writing to the next level? Whether you want to write a memoir, novel, how-to book, or screenplay, *Transformed by Writing* will help you take your project from concept to print and beyond. Get ready to transform your writing and transform your life.

How my life was transformed by writing

As a result of years of reckless living my life and my credit rating were ruined. My credit was so bad I couldn't even open a savings account. Through desperate research and fortunate grace, I discovered some little-known financial techniques and wrote a book called *Credit Secrets: How to Erase Bad Credit*. My life was transformed when the book won first-place in a publishing contest and I became a bestselling author, hitting the talk show circuit and becoming a renowned financial consultant. My most popular book, *Life After Debt*, sold over 100,000 copies and I became the spokesperson for Capital One Financial Corporation based on the success of my subsequent book, *Identity Theft: How to Protect Your Most Valuable Asset*.

After a brief stint in law school, I changed course and earned my Master of Fine Arts in Creative Writing with an emphasis in Screenwriting. I began writing screenplays and adapting books to film and television. I even wrote a comedy script about my experience in law school and adapted my book *Identity Theft* into a feature screenplay about a guy who takes the law into his own hands and goes after the person who stole his identity. But that's another story.

Over the years, I've been involved in more than 10 different films in a variety of roles including writer, producer, assistant director, actor, and stunt driver. Known as the guy who gave legendary filmmaker Cecil B. DeMille his close-up, my movie projects include the epic Cecil B. DeMille biopic (see www.cbdemille.com) based on my novel, *C.B. DeMille: The Man Who Invented Hollywood*. I am also the author of the bestselling book, *Ready When You Are: Cecil B. DeMille's Ten Commandments for Success,* which has transformed countless lives and careers.

Over the years, I've provided creative consulting services to hundreds of individuals, business organizations, nonprofit groups, and governmental agencies including the California State Employment Development Department (EDD) where I developed the online training for Career One Stop Centers based on my book *Blockbuster Resumes: Insider Secrets to Dazzle Your Audience and Blow Away the Competition.* I've appeared on over 300 radio and television talk shows as an expert on a variety of topics including consumer finance, personal achievement, creativity, spirituality, recovery, and Hollywood history.

I recently released my semi-autobiographical novel, *The Light* (New Way Press, 2013), a mystical odyssey that follows Abel Adams, a brilliant but troubled young misfit desperately seeking freedom, love, and spiritual enlightenment while battling drug addiction, dark forces, and strange temptations. *The Light* is a surrealistic adventure tale about redemption and recovery. The book's protagonist, Abel Adams is essentially an allegorical composite of all of us who have gone astray at some point in our lives. I believe that many people will discover their deep identification with Abel's desperate desire for deliverance from darkness. The companion volume is a self-help compilation titled, *Finding the Light Within: A Spiritual Guide to True Peace, Happiness, Freedom and Enlightenment.*

In addition to writing books and making movies, I help others do the same through my work as a creative writing professor and literary consultant. I specialize in helping people become published authors so they can tell their stories and make a difference in the world. People who want to know how to take their writing careers to the next level often approach me for advice. So now I'd like to help you transform your writing and transform your life.

Whether you're looking to write a transformational self-help book, memoir, novel, or screenplay, *Transformational by Writing* is designed to help you tell your story and shine your light in the world.

7 Transformational Writing Secrets

DESPERATELY RUNNING
(from my novel, *The Light*)

Desperately running
Desperately seeking
Desperately dreaming
Chasing the elusive dance
Of a butterfly
As it flutters
Just beyond my grasp
In the sunlight
As it glistens
In my desperate tears
I continue...
Desperately running
Desperately seeking
Desperately dreaming
Till I awaken
To the blinding light
Of reality

To discover that
I am the butterfly
Being chased
As it flutters
Just beyond the grasp
Of the ONE
Desperately running
Desperately seeking
Desperately dreaming
Desperately running
Desperately seeking
Desperately dreaming
□

"We delight in the beauty of the butterfly, but rarely admit the changes it has gone through to achieve that beauty." ~Maya Angelou

What is transformation?

trans·for·ma·tion
/ˌtransfərˈmāSHən/
Noun

1. A thorough or dramatic change in form or appearance.
2. A metamorphosis during the life cycle of an animal.

Synonyms
conversion - metamorphosis - change -

alteration

"Do not conform to the pattern of this world, but be transformed by the renewing of your mind." ~Apostle Paul

Transformational writing is writing that changes lives. Writing coach Christine Kloser, describes the transformational author experience in four levels:

1. Transform yourself – How will your life be different as a result of your writing?
2. Transform your reader – How could you change the life or your reader? What can you say that could positively impact the lives of others?
3. Transform your business – How would becoming a published author and sharing your story change your business or career?
4. Transform your world – How can your book make a significant difference in the world?

What are the Seven Secrets of Transformational Writing?

1. **The secret of meaning** – Every word has meaning. Every story and every action in your story should also convey some kind of meaning.

Not necessary that everything has to be some kind of profound life-changing event, but consider the concept of parables and hidden meanings. Consider ways to add new levels of meaning to your writing. Think about what your stories or your book are really about on the deepest levels. What are the deeper meanings your writing can convey through stories?

2. **The secret of legend** – Joseph Campbell, author of *The Hero With a Thousand Faces* popularized the storytelling concept known as the hero's journey. Also known as the monomyth or metanarrative, the hero's journey is a deeply imprinted story template that connects people from diverse cultures throughout history. Disney studio consultant Chris Vogler developed the hero's journey further in his book, *The Writer's Journey* where he analyzed popular films and broke down the hero's journey into specific story and character elements. There are several variations of the hero's journey, but the basic elements follow the main character (hero) through departure, initiation, and return. The departure begins in the hero's ordinary world, with a call to adventure, a refusal of the call, supernatural aid, and entering the belly of the whale (remember

the story of Jonah). The initiation phase consists of the road of trials, meeting with the mentor, crucifixion, and resurrection (transformation). The return is where the hero demonstrates mastery of both worlds and brings back the reward. Along the journey the hero meets various characters, including the herald, mentor, trickster, goddess, allies, and enemies. There are many variations of the hero's journey, but if you look closely you will see the template in many popular stories and myths. How can you create a larger than life legend in your own writing? Who is your hero?

3. **The secret of vision** – When visionary filmmaker Cecil B. DeMille headed west to make movies in 1913, California was nothing more than "orange groves and desert" and movies were considered a passing fad. He followed his vision and went on to establish Hollywood as the motion picture capital of the world with over 70 major films to his credit. Henry Ford said that if he had listened to what the people wanted, he would have created a faster horse. Instead he invented the automobile, something that nobody knew about or wanted until it was created. When John Bunyan wrote the allegorical classic, *Pilgrim's Progress* in 1678, nobody had ever seen a novel before. What is

something new that you could say or create that nobody has ever seen before?

4. **The secret of showing** – One day Buddha silently held up a flower to the assembly of his disciples. One disciple smiled, understanding completely and became enlightened. Words were not needed. The human brain reacts more to images and stories than it does to explanatory instructions. Think about the early tribal storyteller sitting by the fire describing how a leopard pounced on his younger brother who was walking alone along the dark shaded path under the mango tree and the leopard tore the brother to shreds. Wouldn't that have more effect than simply telling the audience that leopards can be dangerous animals? Show, don't tell. That is the message that I'm always conveying to my creative writing students. Check out the award-winning film, *The Artist* or go online and watch the short film, *Nuit Blanche* for wonderful examples of visual storytelling. While writing your book, even if it's nonfiction, imagine how your stories could be translated into images. How can you make your storytelling more visual and less explanatory?

5. **The secret of releasing** – Many of my greatest writing success have come when I wasn't

looking for them. When I was in my second year of law school I began having second thoughts about my future career. Did I really want to become an attorney? Even though I was still doing well in school, while working a full time government job, I began to wonder whether I had made the right choice. Around that time I received a call out of the blue from a previous publisher who asked me if I could write a book about identity theft. Realizing that my heart was more into a writing career than practicing law, I accepted the assignment and took a leave of absence from law school. I later returned to graduate school, but this time to earn my Master of Fine Arts in Creative Writing. I let go of my plans for a legal career and my writing career took off. This also applies to certain projects after you've done everything you can. Sometimes you just need to let go and move on. What do you need to release in order to take your writing career to the next level?

6. **The secret of silence** – What if you spent less time talking about writing and more time writing? What if you listened more than you talked? Be still and know... Become aware of the still, small voice within. What is the space between thoughts? Learn to listen to the silence. What is the sound of one hand slapping

your face before your grandfather was born in the forest with nobody around to hear it? Take time every day to sit or walk or stand in silence. Whether you call it meditation, silent prayer, or waiting in the stillness, listen for the voice of the inner teacher, the Light that leads you into all truth and wisdom. What does the still, small voice within want you to know?

7. **The secret of action** – Have you ever known someone who is always talking about what they are going to do someday, but they never take any action? I've met many aspiring writers who spend a lot of time talking about their stories and telling people what they are going to do one of these days. I've known others who are always reading books about writing and taking writing workshops and going to writers groups. But they never get their books written. They often start but never finish. Many never get started. I recall telling a counselor that I just checked out half a dozen books on writing from the library and enrolled in a writing class. When he asked me if I started writing anything yet, I had to tell him no. Sometimes the smallest actions can yield the greatest results. Sometimes less is more. Rather than getting overwhelmed with thinking and talking about all these major projects that you don't have time for, take small actions on a

consistent basis. Learn to take baby steps. One word at a time. One page at a time. Five minutes at a time. One day at a time. How can you break your writing into baby steps? What will you write today?

My Creative Process

Within the context of developing and marketing creative writing projects here is my general process: learn, create, improve (edit), promote, wait. Repeat as often as necessary. Learn, create, edit (improve), promote, wait.

Not necessarily one phase at a time or only one project at a time. But, this is the general process that I have used, relatively successfully, over the past couple of decades to write a dozen books, half a dozen film scripts, and production involvement in over ten films. Some books have sold well. Others have not. Some projects come without me looking for them. Others have sprung from deliberation or follow up from previous projects. Everything has a way of working out, in spite of my occasional missteps and sidetracks. I trust the process. But patience is often the overlooked key.

It may not seem to make sense to the outside observer and it may not be the process that works for everyone. But each of us has to be who we are and follow our own paths in accordance with our personalities, experience, and abilities. Of course, it's not just as simple as it sounds and there are many course corrections (improvements/edits) along the way. Progress is not always immediately evident, especially in terms of financial returns, but progress is being made.

I still have more learning, creating, improving, promoting, and waiting to do.

Writing and Recovery

How Stories Transform Lives

In the beginning was the Word. Since the dawn of civilization, the storyteller has held a unique role in guiding, inspiring, and transforming individuals and communities. Every day around the world, in homes, churches, online, through social media, on convention center stages, in theaters, and big and small screens, storytellers continue sharing their experience, strength, and hope by telling others what it was like, what happened, and what it's like now. Whether through listening or telling, writing or reading, stories are powerful. Stories are healing. Stories transform lives.

This chapter focuses on creative writing and recovery with an emphasis on how you can help others transform their lives through writing their stories. You will also discover how you can transform your own life and career by becoming a published author. What's your story?

More of the Mystery of My Story

When you're all alone in the dark you can either close your eyes and go to sleep or look for the light.

After spending more than half my life in and out of jails, rehabs, and prisons while battling drug addiction, I was a dead dog on the road of life. Down in the darkness of death's doorstep, in the depths of despair, the Light began to dawn. Then everything changed.

By the time I entered the recovery house, I was already a successful author, having written several books on personal finance and consumer issues. I had appeared on hundreds of radio and television talk shows as one of the nation's leading credit experts. Writing was an essential part of my life, but something was sorely missing -- my life was still a miserable mess. I needed to do something different. I needed help.

As part of my treatment plan, my counselor arranged for me to write out my fourth step [part of the 12 steps of Alcoholics Anonymous involving writing a moral inventory] in the form of a memoir. For an hour a day I poured out all my thoughts and memories, frightfully surprised as rivers of poetry mixed with secret crimes and lovers bubbled to the surface of my soul and spilled out onto yellow legal pads. The result of this process was a catharsis that led to emotional healing and spiritual insight, transforming my life with a deep and permanent Light.

Within 30 days I had a 300-page memoir in front of me ready to share with the world. I soon found a literary agent who wanted to shop the book to New York publishers as a sensational true confessional. Suddenly, my agent died and the manuscript disappeared into a desk drawer to gather dust. Years later, I dusted off the early draft and decided to change the names, locations, and even the primary character to the point of total anonymity. I recently rewrote the book as a novel titled, *The Light,* a mystical odyssey about addiction, recovery, and redemption.

Writing and Recovery

How many of the 12 steps actually *require* writing? Many people in recovery programs complete workbooks or journals writing out their thoughts and answering questions about each of the 12 steps of recovery. If you sit in enough groups or 12 step meetings or ask a dozen different "experts," you'll get a number of different opinions. According to a strict interpretation of the book, *Alcoholics Anonymous,* the only steps that seem to *require* writing are the fourth step, "Made a searching and fearless moral inventory of ourselves" and the eighth step, "Made a list of people we had harmed and became willing to make amends to them all." The "big book" further indicates, however, that the eighth step is taken from the writing already done in the fourth step. Therefore, one could argue that writing a thorough fourth step inventory is the only writing really required for recovery. But is that really enough?

Regardless of minimal requirements, writing can be an essential tool for discovering deeper layers of emotional entanglements, uncovering destructive thoughts and behavior patterns, and discarding self-destructive habits. So whether a person writes out their daily thoughts in a journal, completes detailed worksheets for each of the 12 steps, pours out poetry on paper, or expands their fourth step into a 300-page memoir, the process of writing is essential to recovery. Writing, as a way to tell stories and express emotions, results in healing and transformation. Words are powerful. Words transform lives.

Freedom Writers

Books like *Alcoholics Anonymous* and *Narcotics Anonymous* are overflowing with the stories of people who have recovered from substance abuse. In the 2007 movie, *Freedom Writers,* Hillary Swank plays a high school teacher who inspires a troubled group of "unteachable" inner-city teenagers to discover tolerance and rekindle their dreams through creative writing. In his stark memoir, *Soul on Ice,* former Black Panther member

Eldridge Cleaver reveals how his life was transformed by writing. Juvenile facilities, jails, hospitals, and prisons throughout the country have instituted creative writing programs to help their residents work through dark emotions, confess their hidden secrets, heal their shattered souls, and transform their lives.

How could creative writing classes be instrumental in today's substance abuse treatment facilities, recovery centers, and sober living homes? If your treatment center, private practice, or recovery facility has not already done so, how might you incorporate creative writing as part of the recovery process? Whether you encourage participants to write their daily thoughts in journals, express themselves with poetry, or tell their stories in longer forms such as memoirs or semi-autobiographical novels, consider ways to encourage storytelling and creative self-expression as an adjunct to your current modalities. You might also look at enlisting a student volunteer from a local college or hiring a creative writing instructor to facilitate weekly classes or work with residents one-on-one. What if you compiled the stories and poems from selected participants into a published anthology? What are some other ways you could incorporate creative writing into the recovery process? What's the best thing that could happen?

What's your story?

Do you have a story that could make a difference in the world? How would becoming a published author transform your business, career or personal life? Are you an expert in your field or have a new perspective on how to solve age-old problems? If you're like most people, you've probably thought about writing a book some day. What's stopping you? What if somebody really needs to hear your story? What if writing your book and telling your own story was part of the healing that you as the healer may need right now? Physician heal thyself.

Getting Started

If you want to build a house, create a business, or develop a new invention, you need to begin with a blueprint. Regardless of whether you want to write the complete book yourself, work with a co-writer, or hire someone else to write the book for you, you will need to start with a concrete description of what your book will be about. Start by brainstorming your ideas. What do you really want to write about? What is the essence of your story? What is your expertise? Who is your audience? What is your tentative title? How do you plan to market and promote your book? Where would it fit on the bookstore shelves in terms of categories and comparable titles? How is it different? After you brainstorm your basic ideas, begin to expand them into a full outline, detailed chapter descriptions, and summary. Create a plan and a writing schedule. Then stick to your plan. Write your book and get it published.

The Hero's Journey

In Joseph Campbell's groundbreaking work, *The Hero with a Thousand Faces,* the hero begins in an ordinary world before receiving a call to adventure. Reluctantly, s/he enters a new world, faces challenges, enemies, allies, and mentors, before crossing the final threshold, facing the ultimate challenge, and returning home with the reward.

Prepare to embark on your personal hero's journey. Your quest is to become a published author so you can tell your story and make a difference in the world. This is your call to adventure. Now begin.

"Whatever you do, or dream you can, begin it. Boldness has genius and power and magic in it."

~ Goethe

How to Become a Published Author

I'm often asked about what it takes to get a book published. Many people start with questions like, "How do I get an agent?" or "How much money can I make for my book?" When I ask them whether they have a book already finished, edited and ready to go, the answer is usually, "No. I haven't started yet. But I have this really great idea and I know it will be a bestseller." OK, right.

So my first suggestion to anyone wanting to become a published author is to write your book first. Or at least create a complete book proposal, which consists of an outline, sample chapters, marketing analysis, comparisons and contrasts with other similar books (and please don't say there is nothing like it), your author bio, and marketing plan (including your platform).

Your book roadmap

Your book roadmap will help you get started by giving you a roadmap to your final destination.

If you want to take a journey, you need to begin with a map to where you want to go. Regardless of whether you want to write the complete book yourself, work with a co-writer, or hire someone else to write the book for you, you will need to start with a concrete description of what your book will be about. Decide that you will begin writing your story today. Not tomorrow. Not next week. Today. Start now by reading this section and using it as a guide to create your book roadmap.

Here are seven steps to creating your book roadmap:

Step 1 - Brainstorm your book ideas.

Take out a notepad or use your computer to write down as many book ideas as you can in less than three minutes. Let your imagination go free and don't censor any ideas at this point. Just write down whatever comes up. Even if you think you are sure about the book you want to write, brainstorm as many ideas on what you want the book to include. Use the phrase, "What if....?" to open up your thinking. For example, "What if you changed your autobiography into a novel?" "What if you taught people a new way to solve their problems?" Ask yourself why you want to write this book and who you are writing it for? What do you hope to accomplish? What is your unique perspective? Consider your experience, your expertise, your imagination, and your dreams. Consider your audience. Whom do you want to reach and why?

Step 2 - Decide what kind of book you want to write.

Is it fiction or nonfiction? In other words, are you writing a novel? Or is it non-fiction such as a memoir, biography, textbook, cookbook, how-to, or self-help book? Are you an expert in a certain subject? What do you know about that you can share with others? What is the story that you really want to tell? Do you have certain life lessons that you have learned from personal experience that would benefit others? Think about the kind of books you love to read. Write a book that you would want to read.

Step 3 - Describe your book in one sentence.

Look at the *New York Times* Best Seller List book descriptions (you can find this on Amazon.com). In order to sell your book, you need to be able to give people an idea of what it's about in a single sentence. This process will also help you to stay on track when writing the book. If you're writing a novel, for example, tell us who the main character is and what challenge they are facing. In a how-to book, simply tell us what the book will teach us how to do.

Step 4 - Create a catchy title.

Give your readers a good idea of what your book is about. Remember that you can change the title later. For now, you just want to have a working title, to keep you focused on the kind of book you will be writing. You can also use a subtitle to give a more complete description. For example, if you are writing a how-to book to help jobseekers, a title such as my popular *Blockbuster Resumes: Insider Secrets to Dazzle Your Audience and Blow Away the Competition* clearly tells readers what this book will do for them and why they should buy it.

Step 5 - Write a three-sentence outline.

Think about a three-act play. Simply describe the beginning, middle and end. Where does the book start? How do you introduce the reader to your main subjects or characters? The middle is where you pour on the action in your novel or give the reader more detailed information about your subject. The ending is where you bring it all together and tie up the loose ends. It might also be good idea to end with the hint of a sequel or more to come.

Step 6 - Develop a more detailed outline.

Here is where you flesh out more specific information about your book. What are the step-by-step processes you want to describe to your reader? The Hero's Journey model of storytelling was popularized by Joseph Campbell in his book *The Hero with a Thousand Faces* and later used as a template for many Hollywood movies, including *Star Wars, The Wizard of Oz* and *Harry Potter*. This is a formula that is based on powerful stories throughout history and throughout various cultures. There are many variations on this formula but the good news is that you can create your own. What are the actions your hero's journey? Start with a one-page outline. Then expand it by adding more detail to every step.

Step 7 - Revise your roadmap.

Take another look at your detailed outline. Does it make sense? Does it describe the book you want to write? Is something missing? Take a break and come back to it with a fresh look before making your revisions. Continue revising until you are satisfied that you have the blueprint for the book that you really want to write.

Now What?

Congratulations! Now that you have your book roadmap you are closer than you've ever been to realizing your dream of becoming a published author. Are you ready to take the next steps?

The Writing Process

I strongly believe in starting with an outline to use as a roadmap or blueprint as I mentioned previously. You may be one of the few successful writers who can just start writing and keep going without knowing how your book will end. If that's the case, go for it. But most people I know who start without an end in mind, never finish. Or they get halfway through and decide they need to start over again. So my advice is to start with your book roadmap as described earlier and save yourself time and heartache.

Set a goal for when you want to finish your book. I've written books in as little as a few weeks. Others have taken me years to complete. When I get on a roll I become obsessed about a subject or story, immerse myself in the topic, and continue for hours and hours each day regardless of outside distractions until the first draft is done. Then I go back and rewrite and rewrite and rewrite. Then revise, edit, proofread, and rewrite some more. Then more rewriting. Your process may be different.

My wife, Lesa Hammond, got her first book

done by using the method she describes in her book, *Achieve in 5! Transform Your Life in Just 5 Minutes a Day* (New Way Press). By dedicating five minutes every day she outlined, wrote, revised, and ultimately published the first in her children's book series titled*, The Thompson Twins: Las Vegas Adventure* as well as *Achieve in 5!* Others schedule a few hours a day early in the morning or late at night when the outside distractions are minimal. Another process is to set a minimum page limit per day until you get through your initial draft. If you wrote one good page a day you would have a 365-page book at the end of a year. Author Tim Ferris talks about writing "two bad pages a day" as part of his writing process. By setting the two bad page minimum, he gives himself permission to write more, but doesn't beat himself up for doing less.

Another technique that many authors have found is to dictate your story or book into a digital recorder and then having it transcribed and later edited. I use the Internet Transcribers service to transcribe some of the teleseminars and radio interviews that went into the making of this book.

After completing an initial draft of your book, go back and read through it to see that it contains all of the main points that you wanted to cover. Does it tell the complete story? Do you include all the facts and information that you want to convey to your reader? Now you are ready for the revision process. You will need to write and rewrite and revise and revise several drafts before you are even ready to give it someone else for review. You may want to work with a writing partner, a writing group, hire a professional editor or work with a literary consultant to guide you through the process. But you are now well on your way.

You have to find a system that works for you. The main thing is that you get started and then keep at it until you have reached your finish line – a published book.

Finding the Right Publisher

What's your book about? Who is your target audience? What other books can you compare it to? Take a walk through your local independent bookstore or major chain and find the section where your book would fit. What are some other similar titles? Take a look at the publishers for the kinds of book you want to write. As you can probably guess, the big publishers may be harder to reach than the small independent presses. One of the biggest mistakes new authors make is to send their book unsolicited to publishers who don't even publish the kind of book they have written. Be sure to know your audience before you begin submitting your book and have it turned down. Find the publishers who publish the kind of book you want to write and become familiar with their policies. Read their books and know what kind of authors they work with. Keep yourself open to the possibilities.

Do you need an agent?

If you want to reach the bigger traditional publishers, your best bet is to submit your book proposal through an established literary agent. Publishers are so swamped with submissions that they want to know that someone else has done the vetting and weeding out of manuscripts that are not in their league. The agent works for a percentage (usually 10-15%) of the book sale price and royalties. The catch-22 is that getting an agent without having been published is not easy and it's not easy getting published without an agent. But there are other ways to get your book published without an agent or having to deal with the traditional publishing system.

Traditional vs. Self-Publishing

After you develop your outline, you can now decide how you want to proceed. Do you want to look for a traditional publisher who can get your book in bookstores and on promotional tours? Or do you want more control and want to publish your book yourself? Is there something in between? I've experienced both and each option has its pros and cons.

Here are some of the main pros and cons of traditional publishing vs. self-publishing:

Money up front – Traditional publishers may pay you an advance against future royalties. That means they could write you a check when you sign the contract with another payment due upon completion of the "acceptable manuscript" and then deduct that advance from any royalties received from future book sales. Unfortunately, unless you are a top name author like Stephen King, John Grisham, or Dan Brown or a big celebrity with a built-in following of millions of potential readers, even the biggest publishers have been cutting down on advances. So don't get your hopes up of getting a million dollars for your sensational life story or vampire novel. Many traditional publishers do not offer advances at all now. Some are even asking authors to do their own copyediting, formatting, and marketing.

With self-publishing you won't get any money up front and you may actually have to pay money to develop your book, including cover design, editing, formatting, proofreading, and consulting services. But you could receive up to 70 percent of the money received for every book sold. In some cases, a self-published book does so well that traditional publishers may offer to purchase the rights for distribution under their brand. Examples include: *The Shack, The Christmas Box* and others.

Control – With traditional publishers you have very limited control over when the book is published. From the time you submit your completed and edited manuscript, it may be anywhere from six months to two years until you see the book in print. With self-publishing you can upload your book into Kindle or other e-book formats as well as print on demand publishing within a matter of days from the time of submission. With self-publishing you also have the ability to make quick changes and reprint corrections and updates within a matter of days instead of having to wait for another print edition.

Distribution – One of the biggest advantages of traditional publishers is their ability to get your book into most of the independent bookstores as well as the big chain bookstores like Barnes & Noble. Many bookstores are averse to carrying self-published books because of the cost of returning unsold copies as well as the generally poor quality of most self-published books. But talk to your local independent bookstore owners and establish a relationship. They can help you tremendously in terms of telling you about what sells and what to avoid. Your small independent bookstore can also become a good friend and help set up book signing and other promotional events once your book is published. On the other hand, so many people are buying books through Amazon and other online retailers that your self-published book can get to the bestseller list without even being in bookstores. Of course, that takes a great deal of marketing and coordinated publicity to get your book noticed in the growing sea of titles.

Royalties – Traditional publishers will pay royalties of usually between five and fifteen percent of net receipts (wholesale price) So if your book sells for about $15 in paperback and $10 wholesale, you may expect anywhere from fifty cents to a dollar fifty for each copy sold. If your book sells 10,000 copies, you might receive $10,000 in royalties (after paying back the advance if you had one) With self-publishing you set the price for the book and can receive up to 70 percent of the royalties, depending on what arrangements you make for distribution. Amazon is the most popular book distributor right now and the process for getting your book self-published is relatively quick and easy.

Chances of getting published – Traditional publishers are looking for books that they know will turn a good profit. That means they need to sell at least 10-20,000 copies to break even. In order for them to consider your book proposal you need to already prove that you have a built-in audience. This is what is known as your "platform." Traditional publishers are usually only interested in new authors that already have an established business, or online presence, or are a recognized celebrity or expert in your field with at least 10-20,000 people on your mailing list. If you don't have such a platform, even the best book proposal may be passed by.

Fiction vs. Nonfiction - Fiction is a much harder sell, especially for unpublished authors. But if you have a story to tell you need to be true to yourself and your story. If you want to turn your story into a movie or television series, you might have a much better chance if you start with a published book first. From personal experience, I can tell it's a lot easier to get producers to read a published book than a screenplay, especially if your book is getting buzz and hitting the bestseller lists.

If you have a strong brand and a powerful concept for a new way of doing things, self-help and how-to books are usually the best opportunity to break in as an author. With self-publishing, you can use your book to establish yourself as an expert in your field and build your brand. Or you can tell that story that you really need to tell to the world. Maybe you just want to leave a legacy behind for your family and friends. I recently heard the story of a financial planner who self-published his book on retirement and sold it as an online eBook. Even though he didn't sell very many copies, he gained hundreds of new clients and made hundreds of thousands of dollars, establishing himself as the go-to guy for people looking to retire.

Other Alternatives

Traditional publishing and self-publishing both have some great pros and some distinct disadvantages. On one hand, many people would love the prestige of being published by one of the big companies and seeing their books in all the big bookstores. On the other hand, you have a much better chance of just writing and publishing your book yourself and going directly to independent booksellers or putting it on Amazon through CreateSpace and other online retailers.

However, with self-publishing there are out-of-pocket costs involved, as well as the effort on your part of getting your book proofread, copyedited, cover designed, formatted, and put on the market.

Another alternative is to find a cooperative or collaborative independent small publisher who can help guide you through the process of getting your book written, designed, edited, formatted, and marketed. Many publishing companies, including some of the larger traditional publishers, are now offering collaborative publishing agreements where they provide specific services and the author pays a portion of the up-front costs.

10 Writers Who Changed the World

"For prophecy never had its origin in the will of man, but men spoke from God as they were carried along by the Holy Spirit." (2 Peter 1:21)

As the bestselling book of all time, the Bible has stood the test of time, having been read, studied, scrutinized, critiqued, and analyzed by more people than any other book in the world. Hundreds of Bible prophecies have come true long after their authors' death. Most of all, the Bible is unique in all the world's literature as a collection of 66 books, written on three continents, by 40 different authors of varied backgrounds (including a fisherman, tax collector, king, military general, prime minister, and physician,) over a period of 1500 years, in three different languages (Aramaic, Hebrew, and Greek.) What other book can make such claims?

The purpose of this chapter is to present selected Biblical writing as unique examples of transformational writing. It is not my intention here to debate the veracity of the Bible, with long deliberations about bibliographical, archeological, and historical evidence. Rather, my focus is on specific authors as to their unique writing styles in the context of transformational writing.

Out of the 40 known biblical authors, this chapter includes the work of ten writers - five from the Old Testament and five from the New Testament. Each of these authors was chosen specifically, not only for their unique writing styles, but also to contrast their differences and similarities in writing toward a common theme – the rebellion of humanity against God through Adam and the reconciliation of humanity and God through Jesus Christ. A hero's journey.

Setting aside the question of whether the Bible represents the inspired words of God, the ten writers included in this chapter have all contributed exceptional literary works to society. From the Old Testament: Moses, Isaiah, Jeremiah, Daniel, and Micah. From the New Testament: Matthew, Mark, Luke, John, and Paul.

Moses begins Genesis, the first book in the Bible, with the words, *"In the beginning, God created the heavens and the earth"* (1:1) and uses a variety of literary devices. The author uses vertical and horizontal parallelism to present alternate accounts of the creation of the world. He combines lyrical prose narrative and poetry to narrate the unfolding of human history, with particular emphasis on the nation of Israel, setting the stage and establishing the lineage for the ultimate coming of the Messiah (also known as Christ or "anointed one.")

Isaiah uses various literary devices such as personification, vivid imagery, sarcasm, alliteration, and assonance to unveil the power of God's wrath for humanity's rebellion and His plan for salvation. As recounted most familiarly in the immortal symphony, "Handel's Messiah," Isaiah provides a stunning prophecy of the coming Savior:

> *"For unto us a child is born, unto us a son is given: and the government shall be upon his shoulder: and His name shall be called Wonderful, Counselor, The mighty God, The everlasting Father, The Prince of Peace." (6)*

The book of Jeremiah is the longest book in the Bible and combines prose and poetry, noted for its stylistic symbolism, alliteration and assonance. Like other prophets, Jeremiah foretells the coming of the Messiah in Chapter 23:

> *"Behold, the days come, saith the LORD, that I will raise unto David a righteous Branch, and a King shall reign and prosper, and shall execute judgment and justice in the earth." (5)*

Daniel writes his prophetic work with vivid imagery and symbolism. In Chapter 7, he reveals this apocalyptic vision:

> *"I saw in the night visions, and, behold, one like the Son of man came with the clouds of heaven, and came to the Ancient of days, and they brought him near before him And there was given him dominion, and glory, and a kingdom, that all people, nations, and languages, should serve him: his dominion is an everlasting dominion, which shall not pass away, and his kingdom that which shall not be destroyed." (13-14)*

Micah wrote a collection of short prophetic messages. Most notably, he predicted the birth of the coming Messiah in Bethlehem.

> *"But thou, Bethlehem Ephrathah, though thou be little among the thousands of Judah, yet out of thee shall he come forth unto me that is to be ruler in Israel; whose goings forth have been from old, from everlasting." (5:2)*

The New Testament begins with four books by Matthew, Mark, Luke, and John. Each of these books (also known as the "gospels") expounds

John's gospel stands in marked contrast to the previous three accounts in its flowery discourses and explicit "signs" and miracles. Like Genesis, John starts his account with "In the beginning…" and spins a sublime description of the divine incarnation. John is known for one of the most familiar verses of the Bible:

> *"For God so loved the world, that He gave His only begotten Son, that whosoever believeth in Him shall not perish, but have everlasting life." (3:16)*

Paul is self-described as a learned man, a Hebrew Pharisee, and Roman citizen. In his letter to the Romans, he addresses the church at Rome, with a symphonic description of God's plan for salvation. Unlike previous writers, Paul's letter is more of a theological treatise, emphasizing the foundations of Christian doctrine, most notably, salvation by grace alone, through faith in Jesus Christ. "For whosever calls on the name of the Lord shall be saved." (10:13) The author waxes eloquently when he describes the condition of those who have accepted the grace of God through faith in Jesus Christ:

> *"For I am persuaded, that neither death, nor life, nor angels, nor principalities, nor powers, nor things present, nor things to come, nor height, nor depth, nor any other creature, shall be able to*

separate us from the love of God, which is in Christ Jesus, our Lord." (8:38-39)

Each of these authors provides a unique style and perspective on a grand epoch, bringing together history, poetry, allegory, and prophecy to tell the universal metanarrative of humanity's creation, fall, and redemption. Do these authors speak on the literal behalf of God, as mere pens in the hand of the Almighty? Or did they write from their subjective realities, revealing their personalities and personal experiences in relation to their respective times and cultures?

Again, debating the historical and bibliographical proofs of the Bible is far beyond the scope of this book. What is beyond dispute, however, is that these writings have survived and flourished for thousands of years and have transformed more individuals than any other writings in the world. What other writers have had a greater influence on the history of the world? What other books have inspired you? What are some other inspired writings that have made a difference in your life?

What if the same spirit which inspired the writers of Old and New Testament times was present as the Light within and all around you here and now? Could there be a continued revelation of divine inspiration written for the modern age? What if…?

The Bible as Blockbuster: The Influence of Cecil B. DeMille's Biblical Epics

"Give me two pages from the Bible, and I'll give you a motion picture." ~ Cecil B. De Mille

Cecil B. DeMille was a born showman, one of the most prolific and successful directors of all time, and the man who was most responsible for turning Hollywood into the world's film capitol. As the creative force behind Paramount Studios, DeMille "handled every existing film genre and formulated some that never existed before" (Katz, 366), most notably the Biblical epic.

In 1923, Hollywood was on the brink of moral implosion, rocked with scandals like the murder of William Desmond Taylor and Fatty Arbuckle's arrest for child rape and manslaughter. America was still reeling from the devastation of World War I, mourning the loss of its sons in the War to End All Wars. Cecil B. DeMille, having already made forty-one motion pictures brought forth his original version of *The Ten Commandments,* a spectacular event unlike any other film before its time.

In preparation for the filming of *The Ten Commandments* DeMille sent a copy of the Bible to every employee with the words, "As I intend to film practically the entire book of Exodus…the Bible should never be away from you. Place it on your desk, and when you travel, stick in your briefcase. Make reading it a daily habit." (Higham, 111-114).

Jeanie Macpherson, who developed the story into two parts, wrote the screenplay. The first part was a retelling of the story of the Exodus, where Moses led the children of Israel from the oppression of Egyptian slavery to the edge of the Promised Land, culminating in the parting of the Red Sea and the giving of the stone tablets containing Ten Commandments from Moses' encounter with God on Mt. Sinai. The second part was a contemporary Cain and Abel story about two sons of an ultra-religious mother, both of whom fall in love with the same woman. The youngest son rejects the Commandments and sets out to break every one of them, while the eldest son strives to live according to God's law. In a memorandum to DeMille, Macpherson wrote:

> *As the sins of Pharaoh and his horde of horsemen are avenged by the down-crashing waves of the Red Sea, which*

> *parted to let the Children of Israel, with their clear faith, pass through, so does the emotional Red Sea engulf our modern [antagonist] Dan McTavish, who has attempted to raise his puny voice against immutable laws. (109-110).*

DeMille filmed *The Ten Commandments* on the sand dunes of Guadalupe, California, using a literal "cast of thousands," including 600 chariots, and hundreds of trained animals. For many people this was the first time they had seen the Bible come to life. With limited access to movie theaters in rural areas, churches screened the film across sheets during special services and social events. The parting of the Red Sea was the greatest film spectacle the world had ever seen.

In 1926 DeMille handed Jeanie the worn family Bible, which his father had used, and gave her what he, referred to as "the most important assignment of her life." He instructed her to follow the great drama of the Gospels to the letter, patently rejecting her idea to frame it with a modern counterbalance. As he did during the production of *The Ten Commandments,* DeMille sent copies of the Bible to every member of his staff, ordering them to memorize every word of the Gospels, and holding daily Bible studies. His research team "explored twenty-five hundred volumes and fifty thousand feet of documentary film [condensing them]...for Jeanie and her own assistants to examine." The cameraman Peverell Marley was instructed to study hundreds of biblical paintings, particularly those by Gustave Dore and Rubens. (Higham, 160-161).

On August 24, 1926, the first day of shooting, DeMille invited members of the clergy to offer their blessings. In his introductory remarks, he proclaimed:

> *We are on the eve of a very vital thing to the world. So far as I know, it is the first time in history that a group such as this has gathered informally to bless an undertaking. In this little group are represented the great religions of the world, all centered on one point – the life, philosophy, and teachings of a great man. No matter whether you believe God descended to mortality or mortality rose to Divinity – His life is an open book – no matter what belief, everyone believes this One man has done a great thing for humanity. We want to give His Work renewed force and vigor and spread it to all parts of the world in order that His motives and sincerity may be understood. We have asked representatives of each faith to give us their good thoughts that the right*

message be given. Thought means so much – hold for us the right thought to help us do our bit toward spreading the great gospel that this great man taught.

Rabbi Magnin of the Jewish organization B'Nai B'Rith, congratulated DeMille on the production, stating:

A great story is bound about a great man to bring about love and peace. Yet this one who has preached love and peace has been the center of such controversy that streams of blood have flowed to the sea…This story free from any theology, will bring home to the world the true message that the great teacher taught through visual education.

Grauman's Chinese Theater opened with the premiere of *King of Kings* and the film enjoyed wide public acclaim.

Billy Graham acknowledges *King of Kings* as a profound influence, calling DeMille "a prophet in celluloid". Graham's daughter Anne Graham Lotz credits the film as being a catalyst for her childhood conversion to Christianity. ABC continues to broadcast the film every year during the Passover week to consistently high ratings

(Mitchell, 6). In the filmed introduction to the 1956 version of *The Ten Commandments* DeMille stated, "The theme of this picture is whether men are to be ruled by God's law or whether they are to be ruled by the whims of a dictator like Rameses. Are men the property of the state or are they free souls under God?"

Many critics found DeMille's moralizing obvious and heavy-handed. Robert S. Birchard, in his article, "Cecil B. DeMille Vs. The Critics," argues that DeMille's anti-Communist politics played a part in his critical response, noting, "it simply wasn't fashionable for the political left to acknowledge Cecil b. DeMille as anything more than a bourgeois capitalist vulgarian." This despite the fact that DeMille's "The Volga Boatman" was well received in the U.S.S. R. as being sympathetic to the Russian Revolution.

In his autobiography, DeMille wrote, "I respect responsible criticism. What I deplore in many critics is not that they criticize, but that they do not see."

In a memo to Louis B. Mayer, movie mogul David O. Selznick confessed:

> *However much I may dislike some of his [DeMille's] pictures from an audience standpoint, it would be very silly of me, as a producer of commercial motion pictures, to demean for an instant his unparalleled skill as a*

> *maker of mass entertainment, or the knowing and sure hand with which he manufactures his successful assaults upon a world audience that is increasingly indifferent if not immune to the work of his inferiors. As both professionally and personally he has in many ways demonstrated himself to be a man of sensitivity and taste, it is impossible to believe that the blatancy of his style is due to anything but a most artful and deliberate and knowing technique of appeal to the common denominator of public taste. He must be saluted by any but hypocritical or envious members of the picture business (Behlmer, 400).*

DeMille's 1956 remake of the *Ten Commandments* was the largest and grandest motion picture made up until that time, with 1200 storyboards, a 308-page script and 70 speaking parts. Historian Sumiko Higashi called DeMille's remake of *The Ten Commandments* an "antimodernist historical film for today's postmodern culture."

DeMille gave formerly blacklisted actor Edward G. Robinson a new start, essentially rescuing his career. In his autobiography, *All My Yesterdays* Robinson wrote, "Cecil B. DeMille returned me to films. Cecil B. DeMille restored my self-respect." DeMille also gave immigrant Ayn Rand a part as an extra to give her a hand in being established.

DeMille employed more women behind-the-scenes in well-paid professional positions than any other filmmaker, including writer-scenarist, Jeanie Macpherson, film editor, Anne Bauchens, and aide de camp, Gladys Rosson. He was also explicit in his depiction of the mixed-race relationship between Moses played by Charlton Heston and the Ethiopian princess played by black actress, Esther Brown (Mitchell 4).

DeMille pioneered the Biblical epic. *The Ten Commandments* (1956) was the most successful and best-known film of its era. During the 1950's and early 60's many of the stories from the Old Testament were put on the big screen and were among the highest grossing films of that period. Biblical epics such as *David and Bathsheba* (1951), *Solomon and Sheba* (1959), *David and Goliath* (1960), and *Sodom and Gomorrah* (1963), dominated the box office.

The New Testament did not present as much romance and physical action as many of the Old Testament stories, and neither DeMille's *King of Kings* nor director George Stevens' *The Greatest Story Ever Told* (1967) received as much critical or box office success. However, several fictional stories involving the life of Christ including *The*

Robe (1953), *Quo Vadis* (1951), and *Ben Hur* (1959) were hugely successful. In 1966, Pier Paolo Pasolini filmed *The Gospel According to Matthew* in Southern Italy with nonprofessional actors and, despite the Marxist director's admitted atheism, the Pope praised the film for its scriptural accuracy.

During the '70s and '80's true Biblical epics fell out of fashion due to the change in social climate, and some controversial films such as the musical *Jesus Christ Superstar* (1973), the parody *The Life of Brian* (1979), and Martin Scorcese's *The Last Temptation of Christ* (1988) suffered dismal box office losses. In 2004, Mel Gibson's independently produced *The Passion of the Christ* made film history as one of the highest-grossing films of all time. *The Passion of the Christ* revived Hollywood's interest in the Biblical epic and several studios have now dedicated divisions to producing faith-based films. However, Cecil B. DeMille deserves credit for creation of Biblical epic as a genre that has had a major effect upon the film industry and millions of individual's lives.

Behlmer, R. (Ed.). Memo from David O. Selznick. New York: The Viking Press. (1972).

Birchard, Robert, S. Cecil B. DeMille Vs. The Critics. In *L'Eredita DeMille (The DeMille Legacy)* Pordenone: Edizione Biblioteca dell'immagine. 1991.

Braudy, Leo and Cohen, Marshall. (Ed.). Film Theory and Criticism 6th Edition. Oxford: 2004.

Higashi, S. Cecil B. DeMille and the American Culture: The Silent Era. University of California Press. Berkeley: 1994

Higham, C. Cecil B. DeMille. New York: Charles Scribner's Sons, 1973.

Katz, Ephraim. The Film Encyclopedia, 5th Edition. New York: Harper Collins, 2005.

Mitchell, Lisa. Legacy. www.cecilbdemille.com/legacy.html

Once Upon a Time in Hollywood

Cecil B. DeMille was the most powerful moviemaker Hollywood has ever known, famous for such epics as *The Ten Commandments, Cleopatra, The King of Kings,* and the *Greatest Show on Earth.*

Before C.B. DeMille made his fateful trip from New York in 1913, Southern California was nothing more than orange groves and desert, with a few scattered ranches and barns and dirt roads. A prohibitionist real estate developer named Horace Wilcox and his wife, Daeida founded Hollywood in the late 1880's. Horace was a religious man who wanted to form a community of like-minded, clean living folks free from the corruption of alcohol and jazz music.

DeMille was born in 1881 to an Episcopal lay minister-turned dramatist and Jewish mother who ran a girl's school. After his father's death, when he was 12, DeMille attended military school. His mother's school for girls floundered and she started a theatrical booking agency. His brother,

William became a successful Broadway playwright. C.B. DeMille struggled for the next twenty years, working as actor, barely making ends meet.

At the age of 33, DeMille made a decision that would change his life forever. In a fateful meeting with theater producer, Jesse Lasky and glove salesman Sam Goldfish (later Goldwyn), C.B. DeMille was offered the opportunity of a lifetime – to make motion pictures in California. DeMille asked his brother, William to loan him the $5,000 he needed to get started, but William thought the venture was too risky. After all, in 1913, California was nothing more than desert and orange groves. Many people considered motion pictures to be a passing fad. DeMille's business partners decided to take a chance on him and advanced his portion of the initial investment. All DeMille needed was enough money to pay his way to California. His wife Constance supported him and offered to pawn the family silver. C.B. DeMille risked everything, temporarily leaving behind his wife and child in New York, to follow a dream. Because of his dream, what began in an old rented barn soon became the motion picture capital of the world.

DeMille was one of the founders of Paramount Pictures with more than seventy feature films to his credit. During his acceptance speech for the Golden Globe Cecil B. DeMille Lifetime

Achievement Award in 2009, Steven Spielberg described how C.B. DeMille's Academy Award winning film, *The Greatest Show on Earth* inspired him to make movies. He says he went home after seeing the film in 1952 and attempted to reenact the train wreck scene using his model train and an 8-millimeter home movie camera. Spielberg said, "I think what was on my mind when I was risking losing my Lionel train set was me thinking, 'Am I going to get away with this?' he recounted. "That anxiety has been haunting me throughout my entire movie career. Whenever I've tried to tell a risky story, whether it's about sharks or dinosaurs or about aliens or about history, I'll always be thinking, 'Am I going to get away with this?'" He says that C.B. DeMille showed him "how to put a lot of money up on the big screen and then make the studios pay for it."

How to Make Your Dreams Come True

What if you discovered the lost memoirs of legendary director Cecil B. DeMille, hidden away in an old cellar, fifty years after his death? What if those pages revealed life-changing secrets that could transform the destiny of countless lives?

What would you want to know about Cecil B. DeMille? How did he break into Hollywood and begin making movies? Why did he persevere in spite of countless obstacles?

Fortunately for us, C.B. DeMille recorded many of his laws for living that have finally been revealed.

Before Hollywood was even a star on the map and moving pictures were no more than novelties in the penny arcades, a certain man wanted to go out to California to make movies. Back then, movies were just cheap little machines you looked into for five cents where you could see a man taming a lion or a woman doing a strip tease. They called these arcade machines nickelodeons and that's what people thought about when you said you were going to make movies. So imagine what a person might think if somebody asked them to invest five thousand dollars in such a venture.

As you can imagine, back in 1913, five thousand dollars had a great deal more purchasing power than it does now. Adjusted for inflation, it would probably be like asking somebody today for five hundred thousand dollars or something like that. That's crazy.

This certain man asked his brother for five thousand dollars to invest in a twenty-five percent stake in his new motion picture production company. The other partners were a glove salesman and a New York theater producer. This certain man's brother was a successful playwright who thought that five thousand dollars would be lost foolishly if he invested in this venture. "What's twenty-five percent of nothing?" he asked. He answered his own question. "Nothing." And nothing is what he invested in the new company. And nothing is what he received back in dividends.

The certain man was Cecil B. DeMille, the legendary director who pioneered the Biblical epic and ushered in Hollywood's Golden Age. But have you ever heard of Cecil B. DeMille's brother, William DeMille? William was the one who was afraid to invest in Cecil's venture. How much do you think his five thousand dollar investment would be worth today? Who knows? Just to give you a little bit of an idea - one of Cecil B. DeMille's homes recently listed on the market for over twenty six million dollars. What do you think owning the rights to DeMille's seventy motion pictures might be worth today? How much would his share of Paramount Pictures be worth?

The other partners were theater producer Jesse Lasky and Jesse's brother-in-law Sam Goldfish. Sam was a glove salesman. He later changed his name to Goldwyn. They put up the remaining share in the business and were well rewarded for their efforts. You've heard of Goldwyn as in Metro-Goldwyn-Meyer or MGM. But that's another story.

Have you heard the story about the star of DeMille's first motion picture? Dusty Farnum was a successful theater actor when Cecil B. DeMille and Jesse Lasky approached him about starring in their film adaptation of *The Squaw Man*. DeMille offered Farnum the same deal he offered to his brother William. In exchange for starring in the film, DeMille promised to give Dusty Farnum 25 percent of the profits in the film. Dusty turned him down, saying, "No, I'll take my $250 a week. That's a sure thing I can count on."

Steven Spielberg credits C.B. DeMille with helping make his dreams come true. He fell in love with movies after watching Cecil B. DeMille's

Academy Award-winning film, *The Greatest Show on Earth*. During his acceptance speech for the Golden Globe Cecil B. DeMille Lifetime Achievement Award in 2009, Spielberg described how, *The Greatest Show on Earth* inspired him to make movies. He says he went home after seeing the film in 1952 and attempted to reenact the train wreck scene using his model train and an 8-millimeter home movie camera. Spielberg said, "I think what was on my mind when I was risking losing my Lionel train set was me thinking, 'Am I going to get away with this?' he recounted. "That anxiety has been haunting me throughout my entire movie career. Whenever I've tried to tell a risky story, whether it's about sharks or dinosaurs or about aliens or about history, I'll always be thinking, 'Am I going to get away with this?'" He says that C.B. DeMille showed him "how to put a lot of money up on the big screen and then make the studios pay for it."

DeMille's granddaughter, Cecilia de Mille Presley, said that she considers Spielberg, "The DeMille of today. Like Grandfather, he has consistently been able to capture vast audiences. He has had great commercial success without losing his personal vision or compromising his integrity."

Steven Spielberg is not the only person who has achieved his impossible dreams by following DeMille's strategies. I love reading biographies of men and women who have achieved extraordinary accomplishments, both in modern times and throughout history. As I have studied their lives, I have discovered that their successes, too, were realized by actions and attitudes that reflected DeMille's teachings, even though some may have never read his writings or seen his films. Oprah Winfrey, Billy Graham, Morgan Freeman, Tom Hanks, Martin Scorsese, Ron Howard, Edward G. Robinson, Gloria Swanson, and Charlton Heston were all great admirers of Cecil B. DeMille. They achieved their impossible dreams by practicing the very principles that DeMille reveals.

I discovered these principles of DeMille's success while I was working on my Master of Fine Arts in Creative Writing. I later wrote the novel and epic biopic screenplay, *C.B. DeMille* and the self-help book, *Ready When You Are.* What I didn't know at the time was that I had inadvertently applied many of DeMille's principles throughout the years. But by applying all ten of Cecil B. DeMille's Commandments for Success, I see my dreams coming true more each day.

Ready When You Are

EGYPTIAN DESERT, 1955

C.B. DeMille sat in his director's chair, lowering the megaphone from his mouth. Desert winds swept sparkling desert sands against steep cliffs. The saffron sun scattered light and shadows across the shimmering dunes, revealing the Sphinx rising in the distance, and rows and rows of pyramids.

DeMille's daughter Ciddy, naturally pretty, her kind eyes shimmering with the natural wonder and imagination of a young girl, sat next to him. DeMille handed Ciddy his wooden cane, worn by time and use.

He turned to her slowly and asked, "Can you keep an eye on this?"

Ciddy took the cane in her hands and looked at it fondly then looking up at her father. "Oh, you think you don't need it anymore?" she asked.

"Something like that," he said with a twinkle in his eyes.

A young camera assistant kneeled before the camera and clapped the slate. "The Ten

Commandments. Scene 70."

DeMille raised the megaphone back to his mouth. "Action!" he shouted.

Hundreds of horses and chariots galloped along the edge of the cliffs edging down the steep incline. Three cameramen caught the action from different angles.

The chariots descended to the bottom of the steep dunes in clouds of dust. DeMille stood to his feet. "Cut! That was fantastic. Perfect."

Moments later, DeMille looked over to Cameraman #1, raising the megaphone again. "Did you get that?"

Cameraman #1 pointed to what's left of his camera, half buried in the sand. "Sorry, C.B. The camera got trampled in the stampede."

DeMille looked to Cameraman #2. The cameraman looked at the front of the camera and wiped a big clod of dirt from the lens. He looked back at DeMille and shook his head.

DeMille jumped up and ran around frantically waving his arms at everybody, looking up to heaven, desperately pleading with God to save this precious shot. He lifted up his megaphone toward Cameraman #3. "Please tell me your camera is working."

Cameraman #3 smiled and gave DeMille a thumbs-up and shouted, "Ready when you are, C.B!"

C.B. DeMille: Time Traveler

What if legendary Hollywood director Cecil B. DeMille discovered the secret of time travel?

That could explain how the visionary filmmaker recreated the historical accuracy of such epics as *The Squaw Man, The King of Kings, Sign of the Cross, The Crusades,* and *The Ten Commandments.* He was the first director on the west coast to use artificial lights and even parted the Red Sea in glorious Technicolor, not once but twice.

Something happened

In 1913, C.B. DeMille knew nothing about making pictures and Hollywood was little more than orange groves and desert. But after a brief visit to the West Orange, New Jersey laboratory of inventor Thomas Edison, DeMille pawned the family silver and rushed out west. From a rented horse barn, C.B. DeMille along with former glove salesman Sam Goldwyn and theater producer Jesse Lasky made the first feature film and transformed Hollywood into the motion picture capitol of the world. The Lasky-DeMille Barn eventually became part of Paramount Pictures Studios. The rest is history. Or is there more to the story?

Could Cecil B. DeMille be the famous "man in a dress with a cell phone" revealed in the 1928 promotional clip of Charlie Chaplin's film, *The Circus* that recently went viral over the internet?

Imagine Cecil B. DeMille racing through time as he captured images and artifacts from the past and future. Could DeMille actually have witnessed such events as the parting of the Red Sea or the resurrection of Christ? What if he actually traveled into the future and brought back future technology to make his spectacular special effects?

Before his death in 1959, DeMille was working on a film known only as *Project X*. Many scholars believe that this *Project X* held the key to DeMille's revelation of the future.

Is time travel really possible?

According to theoretical physicist Professor Ronald Mallett at the University of Connecticut, time travel is possible using light to bend the space-time continuum. Dr. Mallett, whose groundbreaking research based on Einstein's theory of relativity is documented in his book, *Time Traveler: A Scientist's Personal Mission to Make Time Travel a Reality*. Mallet's book, which chronicles his life story, is in development as a motion picture.

Will Cecil B. DeMille's time-traveling adventures eventually make it to the big screen? According to unnamed Hollywood insiders, the closely guarded project may already be in development. But only time will tell.

An Epic Biopic of Cecil B. DeMille and the Golden Age of Hollywood

Based on the novel, C.B. DeMille: The Man Who Invented Hollywood

LOGLINE: Visionary filmmaker Cecil B. DeMille struggles to bring his epic vision to the big screen against the restraints of his financial backer and the temptations of Hollywood.

TAGLINE: Once upon a time in Hollywood.

PREMISE: Creativity overcomes commercialism.

GENRE: Epic biopic in the vein of *The Aviator, A Beautiful Mind,* and *Walk the Line.*

C.B. DEMILLE is an epic biopic of the pioneering director, Cecil B. DeMille and the establishment of Hollywood as the film capital of the world.

DeMille was a born showman, one of the most prolific and successful directors of all time, and the man who was most responsible for turning Hollywood into the world's film capitol. As the creative force behind Paramount Studios, DeMille handled every existing film genre and formulated some that never existed before, most notably the Biblical epic. DeMille is the story of his struggle to make Biblical epics against the greed of New York moneymen and the allure of California starlets.

While creating a unique portrayal of DeMille, the story also pays homage to his appearance in the Billy Wilder film, *Sunset Boulevard* (Paramount, 1950). Because the majority of DeMille's films and his work centered on Paramount Studios (which DeMille began in a barn along with co-founders Jesse Lasky and Adolph Zukor), the story incorporates the making of such films as *The Ten Commandments* (1923 and 1956 versions) as well as *Sampson and Delilah.*

The central struggle in the film is between director DeMille and producer Adolph Zukor. Whereas DeMille is primarily concerned with making movies, Zukor's main goal is making money. The juxtaposition between diametrical forces of creativity and fear establishes an ongoing conflict. Subplots include relationships with DeMille's other partners Jesse Lasky and Sam Goldwyn as well as DeMille's relationship with his daughter Ciddy (Cecilia), his wife Constance and his two mistresses, scenario writer Jeanie Macpherson and actress Julia Faye. While creating and promoting films espousing Judeo-Christian morality, DeMille struggles with his own sins of adultery, anger, and dishonesty. Hence, we have a story of an ordinary man who overcomes relentless obstacles to become a legend.

READER NOTES:

"The theme of DeMille concerns how we, as human beings, deal with our love of life, family and friends."

"This is the best script that I have read in the past year. There is a whimsy and lightheartedness about the whole piece which makes it a pleasure to read and hard to put down."

"The pace of this script is fast. The action and dialogue flow very well in each scene and set up a compelling visual story."

"The idea of bringing the story of DeMille's life to the screen is extremely intriguing and appealing. It has the potential of exploring a seemingly complicated man and his artistic vision."

How to Write a Hollywood Movie

The following is transcribed from a live class on ***Hollywood screenwriting and the hero's journey****. The video is available on my YouTube link at my website: www.RobertHammondConsulting.com*

Robert Hammond: What if you suddenly woke up and you're blindfolded and tied to a chair? You're struggling, you have no idea where you are. You're struggling, you're trying to get free. You're shaking and shaking and suddenly the whole room starts shaking. And you realize you're in the middle of a giant earthquake. Then you wake up. That was just a dream.

My name is Robert Hammond and welcome to Screenwriting Basics – How to Write a Hollywood Movie. Cecil B DeMille, who was also known as the Greatest Showman on Earth. Martin Scorcese called him, "The Man Who Created the Mythic Landscape, Land of the Spectacular." DeMille invented Hollywood. You may have heard of

Hollywood. Put Paramount Pictures on the map. C.B. DeMille actually made 70 movies, including *The Ten Commandments*. Two versions of it, a silent version and the big version that most of you have probably seen. Movies like *The Greatest Show on Earth* and *Cleopatra*.

What I'm going to talk to you about today is really three things, all about screenwriting. Obviously in the next ten, fifteen minutes I can't tell you everything that I know. I have a Master's of Fine Arts in Creative Writing, emphasis on screenwriting. I teach screenwriting at the college level. I work as a creative executive for a Hollywood producer. I work in the industry. I've written several screenplays. I've worked as a producer. I have several projects in development, including the biopic screenplay of Cecil B DeMille, which hopefully will be seen on the big screen sometime soon.

But what I want to talk to you today about is really the basics of, how do you take those ideas and how do you make a movie? How many of you have watched a movie and you've walked out and you think, "I could have done a better job than that"?

Audience: Many times. More than once.

Robert: You ever thought about what it would be like to be involved in making movies? You ever thought, "Oh, I know a great idea for a movie?" How many people at least have had a part of something that they've seen or they've thought of something that could make a good movie? Whether it's somebody in your personal life, or somebody that you know, or somebody dead, or even something historical.

So, what I'm going to talk to you about today is how to take those thoughts, those dreams, those ideas, and put them onto the big screen. This is what a screenplay looks like, for those of you that haven't seen one. [Holds up script] This is the script for *CB DeMille, the Man Who Invented Hollywood* written by Robert Hammond. On the front I've got my agency and production company's name. In a screenplay, one page equals one minute of screen time. A two-hour movie is 120 pages – a hundred and twenty minutes. A 90-minute movie – approximately 90 pages.

The good news about screenwriting is that every page is pretty sparse. It's not thick with just, long dense text. Movies are a visual medium.

What I want to get into is really three points, because I can only tell you about three main things right now, which are probably the three most important things. I'll tell you everything you need to know. You don't have to spend a hundred thousand dollars in film school to learn it. You'll also have the benefit of knowing probably more than most people with an MFA, or most screenwriters or people who say, "I'm going to write a screenplay one day" or "I'm working on a screenplay." That's half the waiters in Hollywood.

You'll learn how to know that if you have an idea, how to turn that idea into a finished product. Then how to take the finished product – which is the screenplay – and turn it into the actual movie that's on the screen.

So that's three concepts. I've given you a handout that talks about them. Basically, you have to get an idea. What's this thing about? Number two is, you need character and a group of characters. You need people. Whose story is this? Then thirdly, you need the actual story outline, or some kind of plot. What happens?

So it all starts with an idea. Where do you get those ideas from? Cecil B DeMille said, "Give me two pages of the Bible and I'll give you a picture." He would just take true stories, like Moses and the Ten Commandments, or he'd make King of Kings, or the story about Cleopatra, Samson and Delilah – you know, that's what he's mostly known for is those big biblical epics. But he wrote a lot of other stories. He took plays that were on Broadway at the time. He came out to Hollywood in 1913, when there was nothing out here but orange groves and desert. People said, "No, they don't make movies in California." Back then, what a movie was, was actually what they called a Nickelodeon, which is actually like a peep show.

Really, only certain kind of people looked at peep shows. Same people that look at peep shows today. So it wasn't something that they thought there was money in that business.

He actually even asked his brother Henry, "Give me five thousand dollars to invest in this movie business." Henry thought Cecil was crazy. He offered a deal his first actors saying, "I'll give you a percentage of the business if you'll work on a percentage." They said, "No, I want my two hundred and fifty dollars, cash." Little did they know that Cecil B DeMille would make seventy major motion pictures, basically put Hollywood on the map and basically put Paramount Pictures on the map. Basically created the golden age of Hollywood.

So the question is, "What if...?" What if you woke up blindfolded, tied to a chair? What would happen? Then all of a sudden, you're shaking and shaking and shaking - there's an earthquake. Then you hear somebody asking you questions in a voice you don't recognize. "Where's Destiny's Lance?" "What?"

What you do now, however, is - because of who you are, you're a brilliant graduate student. And your thesis is on Destiny's Lance, which is the Spear of Destiny. The one thing you know about that for sure is that the legend says that whoever possesses the lance – whoever possesses Destiny's Lance – will rule the world. You've done the research. You know that that Spear of Destiny is not where they say it is. You've learned, you've uncovered secrets about this lance that, throughout history, has been in the hands of some of the most powerful people in the world: The Emperor Constantine, Attila the Hun, Adolf Hitler, George Patton. But they think you know where it is.

So step two, What if you write a movie about that story? It's taking an idea about anything: something that really happened... Just a thought, someone really posed that question to me one time. They said, "What if you wrote a story about, some day you just wake up blindfolded and tied to a chair?" That was the idea.

I wrote a book several years ago called *Identity Theft: How to Protect Your Most Valuable Asset*. I was in law school at the time and the publisher, who I had worked with previously and had written several books on other consumer-related topics, asked me, "Can you write a book on identity theft? It's the biggest, fastest growing crime in the world." I said, "Sure." I had to take my time off of law school, which is when I ended up writing this book.

It's a true story, a factual book, a how-to book. But I did a lot of research on the Secret Service, the FBI, and all these different terrorist organizations, and criminal organizations. And I just thought, wow, what if you just woke up one day and somebody stole your identity? And all of a sudden, you get calls from people saying, "You owe us all this money." Then you go to work and you end up losing your job, because they think you've got a criminal record. Then your credit cards don't work. All of a sudden your cell phone quits working, because they're saying, "You owe us ten thousand dollars." You're getting people hounding you. You get pulled over by the police and you get arrested for a crime you didn't commit. What if...? Sounds like you have a problem, doesn't it?

Woman: Little bit.

Robert: That's another story. What I did with another movie is I took *Identity Theft* and I took some of the true stories out of there and I said, what if I make up a character and this happens to them? That's how their day starts. They start getting calls. They start getting harassed. They go to work, they lose their job. Everyone turns against them. That's the starting point. So what you need is those "What if?" ideas. You take true ideas. What If they make a movie about this great director, Cecil B DeMille? I haven't seen one. Closest one I've seen like that is *The Aviator,* about Howard Hughes. Which is similar. How many people have seen *The Aviator*?

So what you need in order to make a movie is

not just an idea, because we all have them, we all have ideas. They're going to make a movie about Abraham Lincoln. Yeah, there have been plenty of movies about Abraham Lincoln, but they're still making them. Steven Spielberg is working on a movie right now about Abraham Lincoln. What if we found out that the reason he got assassinated was different from what we thought?

One of the first projects I ever worked on was based on a book titled, *The People vs. Lee Harvey Oswald*. The question was, who assassinated President John Kennedy? What if Lee Harvey Oswald hadn't been killed by Jack Ruby? What if Oswald went into a coma, three years later they bring him out of the coma and now he has to stand trial for the assassination of JFK?

I got the contract from the publishing company, grabbed some other producers, put some money into it and we developed and wrote the script for that. Didn't end up going where we wanted it to go, but it was an interesting idea. It was like, What if we had the trial of Lee Harvey Oswald? You know these conspiracy theories, they say, what if Lee Harvey Oswald didn't act alone? What if all that evidence actually came into trial? What would happen? So again, that's the what if.

What you need to do with those is you need a character. So who's your character? You come up with a name, an identity for somebody that you want your story to be about. What we like is a Hero's Journey. Somebody that's got a problem. A person who wakes up, tied to a chair blindfolded, pretty much has a problem to start out. Someone who gets their identity stolen has a problem, but generally, they didn't start out that way. This person had an ordinary life at one point. So what you want to do is discern, who do you want to hear the story about? Most people, when they write their screenplays or their stories, usually it's about themselves. That's why half the screenplays out there are about a struggling screenwriter, trying to make it into Hollywood. Or a struggling actor who decides to write a screenplay and star in it and he becomes a Hollywood star. Or a struggling government employee who wants to write screenplays and be a movie producer instead of a government employee. So you've got to come up with something different than that! There's too many of those screenplays out there.

Come up with something. Come up with those What Ifs. But then, you need, not just the idea, but you need to develop the character. How old is the character? Is it male or female? There's a big difference between having a character who is a forty-year-old ex-Navy SEAL from New York in the same situation as you have an eighteen-year-old cheerleader from Iowa. So even that same exact story, losing their identity, think about how those two people would act differently in the same situation.

Think about all of these other stories that have actually already happened. You can take stories like Romeo and Juliet and say, What If, instead of these two rich families, these are two gangs? Anyone ever seen *West Side Story*? That's Romeo and Juliet.

So most stories have already been told. The deepest level of story. The reason why we see movies and we say, "That feels so powerful, so familiar." And some people criticize. How many of you have seen *Avatar*? Some people criticized it, "Oh, that's like this." But the thing is, millions and millions of people saw it and they loved it, because it reminds them of something that's deeper than just another story. It's different than just *Dances With Wolves* or *Braveheart.* There's something that's deeper there – that's the hero's journey, that's the storyline. That's the most important thing, besides having an idea, having a character, is taking the story and putting it into three acts: beginning, middle and end. Every story has to start somewhere and it has to end somewhere. The journey is what happens in the middle. The Hero's Journey is a long process. It's what stories and myths are made out of, like Jason and the Argonauts and Homer's Odyssey. Both are mythological stories. True stories, even the story of Moses. Stories of great spiritual leaders.

Even stories of Captain Kirk and *Star Trek.* The story of *Lord of the Rings.* Both are the same Hero's Journey. *Harry Potter.*

You start out basically with your characters and something happens. That person now has problems. Life was normal, but now something happened. And somebody, an antagonist, some kind of bad guy or bad situation has occurred that creates some conflict. Now this person has to resolve it. He added some sidekicks and some mentors. Most of you know you've got someone who's working with them, someone who's a teacher, a coach type of a character. Then, the problem is, this thing gets worse and worse and worse. One of the ways that we look at the three acts is you introduce your hero and you chase him up a tree. Act Two is you throw rocks at him, while he's in the tree. Act Three, you're going to get to the place where everything seems lost. You ever notice in almost any movie you've seen, especially *Indiana Jones* – Spielberg's good at this – everything's falling apart. Bridge is out, you've got people shooting at you, and you're not going to be able to make it. Everything is on fire. You've got bombs dropping, you've got a timer that's going to go off in twenty seconds and the world's going to come to an end. So if you have these high stakes, all these things are going to happen unless you figure it out. The truth is if all this stuff goes off, the hero's going to be dead. James Bond has got a laser cutting up through his... He's going to die.

Except, he's learned something from these mentors. He's gained something through this and he now has remembered or realizes where Destiny's Lance is. He has now answered the question of that story and now the hero overcomes just as all seems lost. That's Act Three. Then he comes back to where it started. Only difference is, everything is different.

Now this hero doesn't have to be some male macho, Navy SEAL. This is *Cinderella*. This is *Alice in Wonderland*. This is *Buffy the Vampire Slayer*. This is any story. Could be a romantic comedy. They all go through basically the same things: we have a good character, and you have to come up with some trait about the character. You know, a stereotype. The person's a computer expert. Don't make the fat guy with glasses the computer expert and he eats Hot Pockets all day. Make it the beautiful young blonde cheerleader who's a computer expert. Somebody you don't expect to do that thing. You change the character around, change the story around, you keep asking this question: What if...?

So again, there are many stories out there. I know you guys have a multitude of creative ideas. This is just a beginning. What's your story?

7 Steps for Outlining Your Blockbuster Movie Script

"A picture is made a success not on a set but over the drawing board." ~ Cecil B. DeMille

A blockbuster movie starts with a great script. A great script starts with a great outline. A great outline starts with a great idea. Here are seven steps for turning your great idea into a blockbuster Hollywood movie script.

Step 1: Brainstorm.
Write down as many ideas as you can in less than three minutes. Let your imagination run free and just write down whatever comes up. Use the phrase, "What if....?" to open up your thinking.

Step 2: Genre
According to The Internet Movie Database (IMDb), the biggest Hollywood blockbusters belong to the following genres: science-fiction movies like *Star Wars* or *Avatar*, action-adventures

like *Indiana Jones* and *Pirates of the Caribbean,* and family-friendly comedies like *Shrek* and *Toy Story.* Think about the kind of movies that appeal to the widest audience.

Step 3: Logline

A logline describes your story in 1 sentence. Look at the descriptions in the online movie guide listings for examples. Be sure to identify your main character, setting, and major conflict. This process will also help you to stay on track when writing the screenplay and make it easier to sell.

Step 4: Title

Give your audience a good idea of what your movie is about. You can always change it later. For now, you just need a working title to keep you focused on the kind of screenplay you will be writing.

Step 5: Structure

Describe the beginning, middle and end of your story in 3 sentences. Where does the story start? What happens? How does it end?

Step 6: Hero

The hero's journey model of storytelling was popularized by Joseph Campbell in his book *The Hero with a Thousand Faces* and further developed by Chris Vogler in his book, *The Writer's Journey.*

The hero's journey is a template for many Hollywood blockbuster franchises, including *Star Wars, Indiana Jones* and *Harry Potter*. This ancient template is based on powerful stories throughout history and throughout various cultures.

Step 7: Revise

Read your outline aloud. Does it make sense? Does it visually describe the story you want to tell? Are your characters believable? Revise your outline until you're ready to start the first draft of your 90-120 page blockbuster script.

Brand Yourself with a Blockbuster Bio

Along with your back cover copy and press release, your author bio is one of the most important pages you will ever write. Who are you? What qualifies you to write this book? What's your story? What problem can you help people solve? These are the questions that go into branding yourself with a Blockbuster Bio.

As you well know by now, I write books, make movies and help other people do the same. As a bestselling author and award-winning screenwriter, I'm known for giving Cecil B. DeMille his close-up with the epic biopic. That's part of my branding process. When people think about Cecil B. DeMille, they think about Robert Hammond. When they think about Robert Hammond, they also think about writing books and making movies. That's how branding works. Formerly I was known as the "credit doctor" or the guy who helped people find "life after debt."

In another reinvention I was also known as the leading expert on identity theft. But now I prefer to be known as the person who can help you become a published author so you can tell your stories and shine your light in the world. That's also what's known as my "elevator pitch" or a short way to describe to people who I am, what I do, and how I can help them.

Since you already know that Cecil B. DeMille was master of the blockbuster movie and the biblical epic, let's now take a look at *Cecil B. DeMille's Ten Commandments for Building Your Blockbuster Bio*:

1. **Know Your Audience** – Who are you targeting? Make sure your bio focuses on the problems your audience wants to solve.
2. **Know Yourself** – What are your greatest strengths and accomplishments? Highlight your achievements up front.
3. **Be Accurate** – Does your bio reflect the true you? Be sure it is free from factual, grammatical, spelling, and typing errors.
4. **Be Brief** – Can you promote your elevator pitch in one sentence? Make sure you have a one-page bio for the back of your book and a shorter version for speaker introductions.
5. **Be Clear** – Is your bio easy to read and understand? Free of jargon and confusing phrases?

6. **Be Amazing** – What are your most notable skills and achievements? What are you most known for?
7. **Be Creative** – How can you come up with a creative way of describing yourself so you stand out from the crowd?
8. **Be Relevant** – Does the information in your bio relate to the topic of your book?
9. **Be Professional** – Is your bio well organized, representing you as a competent author and business professional?
10. **Be Visual** – Does your bio look visually appealing?

Business bio expert Nancy Juetten tells clients to emphasize story elements in order to create a "wow" effect, rather than just listing your experience. Make sure your bio tells your audience a story they will remember.

Take a look at author bios in the back of books that appeal to your same audience. How do these authors describe themselves? Be sure to take a look at the press releases and bio in the back of this book. Your press release is another way of branding yourself by giving a quick pitch about your book, business, newsworthy project, or upcoming event. For more help with bios, branding, and promotion, I've listed some recommended resources in the back of the book.

Good Friday: A Writer's Journey from Prison to Pardon

Transcribed from August 10, 2013 broadcast interview on The Philippe Matthews Show

A Writer's Life

Philippe Matthews: Hey, we're back, ladies and gentlemen, on the Philippe Matthews Show, and today I've got Robert Hammond on the show with me today -- an incredible, incredible gift to the planet -- and we talk about overcoming and reinvention.

This guy is the poster child. He's an award-winning screenwriter, producer, and author of, I think, more than 10 books, and he is just an incredible cat, and someone you absolutely should know and should support.

How are you, my good buddy?

Robert Hammond: Oh, thank you so much, Philippe. It's really great to be here with you.

Philippe: It's awesome to have you. We talked sometime ago, and I just thought that you were a prolific writer -- which you are -- and screenwriter, and writing books like *Ready When You Are: Cecil DeMille's Ten Commandments for Success* and *C.B. DeMille: The Man Who Invented Hollywood,* which you're working on a biopic, which I think is huge.

But before we talk about all of these prolific books and screenwriting, let's talk about you and your background, because you recently sent me an email that personified my middle name, which is "Shock," or my nickname. [Laughter]

Robert: [Laughter]

Philippe: If you recall that email and recall that conversation, let's start there so that the audience can get an understanding of why I feel you are so powerful and gifted, because you have overcome quite a bit.

Robert: Okay. Well, thank you. Thanks so much, I do remember that conversation, Shock. [Laughter]

Philippe: [Laughter]

Robert: But as you kind of alluded, I believe, I'm kind of known in Hollywood and in a lot of places, as like the "DeMille guy," the Cecil B. DeMille guy, or the guy giving Cecil B. DeMille his close-up, because I've been working on the big biopic.

You know, it's kind of like *The Aviator*, a big

movie about -- and the big director. And I've written books, some of them about him, including, *Ready When You Are,* and all that.

Philippe: Mm hm.

Robert: But I've written a lot of other books. However, just recently -- I'll just start at what happened at the end that gave me the reason to contact you and I'll probably be doing some other media later -- I just received a governor's pardon from Jerry Brown and that was on Easter.

Philippe: Easter 2013, so this is huge because I think when people hear about governor's pardon, what does that mean, and then they think about it, and it's like, "Wait a minute!" [Laughter]

Robert: [Laughter]

Philippe: A governor's pardon? I remember that, and it was very controversial. What did you do? So let's take him back through the background, as to what led up to the governor's pardon, which is unbelievable, but you had as many young men, a troubled childhood, to say the least -- an identity crisis, to say the least.

Robert: Yes, absolutely, and that's like the quick story. I mean, I guess if I was going to put the story in a couple words it's be like "the prodigal son." If any are familiar with that. The guy who leaves his family, basically, thinking, "Okay, here, I'll just take what I can get and go out on my own, and do my own thing."

And he just ends up at the bottom of

everything, in the pigpen. The prostitutes, the drugs… I mean, metaphorically, in the prodigal son story, but the pigpen, basically, and just a wild living, and I lived it, through the 60s.

I mean, well, late 60s I got into a lot of things that a lot of people did get into. Not everyone -- and I really have a lot of respect -- and I know, people like yourself, others, who really made an early decision.

"Hey, that I'm not going down that path," and they just didn't do it. You know, they didn't take drugs. I mean, you know, they may have done a few things here and there. I mean, we've all stumbled along the way.

Philippe: Sure.

Robert: But some of us, like myself, just take things to extremes, and I don't want to blame anyone else, but I know I've had a troubled life -- but, actually, I had really wonderful parents.

My father is a doctor. My mother has a Master's in social work, and actually was a teacher and worked at the Department of Health, Education and Welfare, and she was a counselor. So it's not a question… we went to church, and I was in the choir, was a Boy Scout, you know, all the outwardly…

Philippe: If you weren't born in the inner city, you're not from the ghetto, you're not dodging bullets in the streets of Compton, I understand.

Robert: Well, I didn't start out there, but I,

actually, I did do that on my own. [Laughter]

Philippe: You did! [Laughter]

Robert: [Laughter] I ended up in the ghetto and dodging bullets. I mean, literally.

Philippe: But, you know, what I think is interesting, Robert, though, is that there is -- and a lot of people, unfortunately, do now talk about this, and that is the pressure to measure up to this, whatever the household standard is.

Especially if it's high academically, you've got academically accomplished parents. You are probably, at that particular time, you're probably the only young male of color in your neighborhood, or possibly, school.

And so I can absolutely see, because I used to just get picked on because I knew how to speak the English language. So I can only imagine!

Robert: In other words, talking "white," as opposed to black.

Philippe: Exactly! Exactly! So, you know, who knows? You grow up, and you become the Oprah of the Internet, but anyway!

You know, so talk to me about that. Am I on the right track, in terms of that assessment?

Robert: Oh, absolutely, Philippe. That was an issue for me, and again, it's not a question like blaming my parents because, obviously, I mean, my mother still to this day, a lot of stuff -- even when I told her about the pardon a couple of months ago -- she was in tears, as well as I was.

Because she felt so like: "Oh, if only I had done more to keep you from going that way," and it just sort of broke my heart, just thinking that she even thinks that my choices had anything to do with her.

Philippe: Well, the blessing is that she lived long enough to see her son pardoned and see her son…

Robert: She did.

Philippe: So that's the best…that's a goldmine, right there, so I'm sure…

Robert: Oh, absolutely.

Philippe: Yeah.

Robert: They have forgiven me for so much, just the governor's pardon and forgiveness was definitely kind of an icing on the cake.

Philippe: Sure, sure.

Robert: But you know, even that, being just forgiven by God and my parents, and myself -- and that's the hard part, really -- my own personal forgiveness of myself.

Philippe: Absolutely.

Robert: But back to your question. Yeah, we lived in some poverty at times, yeah, because my dad was in college for a while, but he went to medical school.

He was in military, also, and he was an officer so we moved around, and so I had to deal with it, like starting over quite a bit with new friends.

Philippe: Mm hm.

Robert: And trying to fit in... and then, ultimately, growing up in a real small, little suburban town in Central California -- Santa Maria, actually, near Santa Barbara in a really nice area. We lived in a nicer part of that town for a lot of that time when I was growing up.

So it was sort of like me trying to fit in. Many times I was the only black person not only in my class, but in the whole school.

Philippe: Wow!

Robert: And later, my younger sisters came along and then there might have been a couple of Latinos and maybe one Filipino or something.

Philippe: Mm hm.

Robert: You know, here and there, but very, very minimal, particularly in elementary school.

Philippe: Mm hm.

Robert: So that was, I think, part of my confusion, I guess, was just trying to blend in, which you can't make yourself look a different way. [Laughter]

Philippe: Right. Right.

Robert: I tried to impress people. -- I was pretty smart, trying to show off and then, make jokes, and be the class clown and then, ultimately, it was more just getting in trouble.

And so, even though I have my undergraduate degree in psychology and sociology, I really don't quite understand why I did all of what I did.

I just know that, ultimately, I found people

who I could fit in with, especially in the late 60s, which were kind of like the hippies, and the Jimmy Hendricks, Sly and the Family Stone kind of a style, and that sort of crowd.

Philippe: Mm hm.

Did you, in that environment, when we talk about trying to fit in -- obviously, you can't change your skin color -- were you ever bullied, picked on, assaulted, dealt with…

Robert: Yeah.

Philippe: Slurs of the N-word.

Robert: Oh, yeah.

Philippe: Did you have to go through that identity, as well?

Robert: I did. And back then, yeah, in order to give it as being bullied, which I know we talk a lot about that, today. I did have my share of that in my day.

Philippe: Mm hm.

Robert: Some fights, but yeah, I did definitely get called those names and particularly, at times, and I really didn't even know… early on, I didn't even know what they were talking about.

Philippe: Mm hm. You had no frame of reference.

Robert: No, we lived in Washington D.C. for a while. I was born in Virginia, we lived in Washington D.C. You know, it was pretty much an American area, which I wasn't even thinking about things like that at five, six years old.

Philippe: Sure.

Robert: And then we moved to the state of Washington, when my dad was in the military -- a captain in the Army and we moved to Fort Lewis -- and that was when I first experienced that all-white environment. I didn't really even know what that was.

Philippe: Mm hm.

Robert: But I mean I just knew, you know, here I don't look the same, and people start playing with my hair, and kids would call me names.

Philippe: Mmm…

Robert: And even the teacher would say, "Oh, well, you're the colored guy. So, you know, boy. You need to really set an example." I'm like, "What?"

Philippe: Wow!

Robert: And then we would like color with our crayons and I would remember, once when using a black crayon the teacher told me, "Oh, black is a horrid color, so don't use black. That's ugly."

Philippe: Hmm…Mm hm.

Robert: You know, it was just "Oh!" and I was just a little kid. And a little phrase, I would say, "Gee, if I close my eyes, maybe you can't see me."

Philippe: Mmm… Wow.

Robert: I don't know if you know that feeling of just wishing you could just...

Philippe: Yes. Yes.

Robert: I felt like that commercial: "Calgon,

take me away!"

Philippe: Yeah, absolutely!

Robert: I wished that I could just disappear. I'm invisible and let me just not feel what I feel, and I think that all these things kind of tied in.

Again, not to blame that for, "Oh, because of that is why I went down this bad path" because I didn't necessarily…

Philippe: Well, I think there is a connection in terms of that, Robert, and that was wanting to disappear and not be around, and that's huge.

And I think seeking "the bad-boy lifestyle," especially as it relates to drugs and drugs are a way of numbing you.

Robert: Yes, it is.

Philippe: And mitigating, if only temporarily, with of course consequences, the pain that you're in, that really you had, again, no frame of reference, really no one to talk to about it, and here you are a kid coming of age, and what do you do?

Robert: Well, it's always like looking for something. You know, there's something missing in my life I felt I needed. Whether I was trying to fit in or just trying to feel like I knew who I am.

Philippe: Mm hm.

Robert: And have you ever had that experience where you're desperately looking around for your keys in the morning or for your glasses and you're looking all over and just blaming everybody and then all of a sudden you realize you have them in your hand?

Philippe: Right! [Laughter]

Robert: Or, your glasses on top of your head?

Philippe: Yeah, it happens, and unfortunately more frequently than not.

Robert: Yes.

Philippe: [Laughter] but absolutely!

Robert: That's kind of my long story, I would say. [Laughter] And so, I'm looking for something, you know? I just was always blaming, and going here and going there, and whether it was drugs or sex or rock and roll, I mean, I needed to fill up that missing place in myself, I think, and it wasn't a part of myself.

Philippe: So now, was there a point where you were addicted, in terms of the technical term or the clinical term, addicted?

Robert: Yeah, absolutely. Eventually, like I said, things that may have started out kind of just as having a nice time, you know, like a little marijuana and some psychedelic kind of drugs in the late 60s. They had these, you know, peace-love type of thing. But I eventually started taking heroin.

Philippe: Mm hm. Mm hm.

Robert: So it's just seeming like this hero's journey on heroin, just starting that kind of in the normal place, and then entered this inciting incident of this drug here, it was like wow!

Philippe: Mm hm. Mm hm.

Robert: I know Natalie Cole and some others have said similar things, but when I first experienced it, it was like "I'm home. This is heaven, this is Eden." I was like "Wow! Oh!"

Philippe: Yeah, I remember that. As a matter of fact, because I think most times people say that the first time using it, they get just almost deathly ill, which in some situations, curtailed them from using it.

Whereas, when Natalie Cole, when she took it, it was like drinking cold water on a hot summer day. It was just absolutely quenching, and took to it like a fish in water.

Robert: Right, and that was..

Philippe: So that was your experience?

Robert: Me too.

Philippe: Oh, my gosh, so you didn't have a chance in heck, did you?

Robert: No, because it was like I said, by the time I… I mean, it was one of those things that you say, "Here, this is something I'll never do." I mean I knew what they were talking about.

Philippe: Sure.

Robert: I mean I didn't like getting vaccinations, let alone taking a needle and putting it in my own arm, you know?

Philippe: Right, right.

Robert: You know it's like frightening, at one point. But eventually, you know, it's amazing the things that we'll do that we say that we'll never do? I mean, I never thought I would let it go that far.

Philippe: Never say never, it seems like.

Robert: But it was one of those areas that, once I was at that point, I guess with all the other things going on, that it just seemed like the thing to do, and then when I did step over that line, so to speak, then it felt like I found heaven. You know, "this is what I've been looking for."

Philippe: Mm hm.

Robert: This feeling, this bliss so it was a tough road to stop doing it because like the worst charge you'd get…

Philippe: Sure. Sure, so you even went further than that at a result of using. Of course, now you're into this "the culture." Now, you're selling your soul as well.

Robert: Well, yeah, you have to do something at some point, and well, I'll speak for myself because it was kind of expensive. It was not something you can just pick up for like fifty-cents at the corner drug store. So, I mean, spending $5, $10, $20, $100, $200 a day, eventually, or more…

Philippe: Wow!

Robert: Did a lot of things. I sold drugs. I've stole, you know, I was a shoplifter. I was a robber. I carried a gun. I was a drug dealer. I mean, these are just a few different things. You know, I wrote bad checks. I forged things. I created new identities. I did a lot of things. I broke into houses.

I just did horrifying things, and I mean I think I hate to even, when I think about it I'm like, "God, I can't believe that I just did that."

Philippe: Mm hm.

Robert: Yes, but I did all those criminal things many, many years ago, which is why I received the pardon, ultimately. Which was Governor Jerry Brown's way of looking back at the many, many years since then, you know, which happened a long time ago.

Philippe: Sure. Absolutely. Absolutely. I mean, it's obvious that you are completely rehabilitated from that life and lifestyle. When… every person that I've ever talked to that has had any type of substance abuse or addiction, there's always like, an "ah-ha" moment and turning point.

Some have more than one, but usually there's always a turning point. What was your turning point in terms of, "I'm not going to use again. I need to get rehabilitated, I need to stop this," and two, what led up to your eventual incarceration?

Robert: Well, those are good questions. For me, one thing I'd like to say is that hitting bottom is when you really decide to stop digging.

Philippe: Mmm.

Robert: Because I've hit bottom before and said, "Okay, that's it. Never again," and then I've gone back out and done the exact same thing.

Philippe: Hmm.

Robert: I mean I've been puking my guts out over a toilet or laid in the gutters somewhere or just out there in the total despicable, you know, hell holes of jails and said, "Okay, that's my bottom, never again," you know, and that's one of those things that many people I know have gone through.

And one of the things that I guess, that's one thing I just want to kind of pause and say that I really want to give hope to anyone who's gone through things like that. I'm not talking about everyone having to go through the extreme of like heroin addiction or cocaine or speed or things like that.

Philippe: Mm hm.

Robert: But just, your life has gotten so far out of control, whether it's in relationships because I know a lot of people just get in really bad relationships.

Philippe: Mm hm.

Robert: Or they get into really bad lifestyles, and whether it's gambling or just anything that just causes health problems or causes mental problems or causes just emotional problems, and we've all had something that's gone on, and then we stop. We say, "Yeah, I'm not going to do that anymore."

Philippe: Sure.

Robert: And we go do it again. So for me, I'd say the biggest pivotal moment, for me, and like I said, I had numerous ones and then even after this still had relapsed, you know, reminders, was when I was alone, and I was in jail.

You know, this was many years ago, and I was actually told that I was getting ready to die. They said, here -- and I had hepatitis and jaundice -- and speaking of, you know, they'd say "high yellow." [Laughter]

A totally new meaning to that phrase. I mean my eyes are yellow. My liver was shot. I was totally gone, and this was Thanksgiving, and I was like here in jail, totally lost everything.

I had nothing… my family, wife at the time, and just… I hated myself, and the medical people were even saying, "Hey, you're going to be dead by Christmas."

Philippe: Wow!

Robert: So that was around Thanksgiving, and that was… "Okay," giving up. I mean I hated myself. I really didn't want to live. I didn't care, but I was in so much pain and just so much agony that I just gave up, in a sense, and then hat was where… and I use this phrase literally "saw the light."

It was like I talked about before, like you've lost your keys, and you're like running around and, "Okay, where are my keys?" or my glasses.

Philippe: Mm hm.

Robert: And then one day, it's like suddenly it's like, "Oh! Wow!" and it was like hiding in plain sight, and I say that in the sense, I'm not talking like just some religious experience. I mean, although you could call it that.

Philippe: Mm hm.

Robert: Like one of these things that William James said about the varieties of religious experience, where people have different ways of coming to this place. It's not just a belief system.

It's not just a ritual, stepping up, walking the aisle and saying a certain formula. It was really a literal, spiritual light.

Philippe: Wow!

Robert: It was like "Wow!" I can see. And that's one of the reasons I actually wrote the book called *The Light,* which originally was like a -- we'll probably talk about it later, but just to mention it -- that *The Light* was originally an autobiography.

I really, eventually, had to just talk about all that and go back to my life, and I could really see it. I just saw things very differently, and that's when I say -- talk about light -- we're not just talking about artificial light or natural light like sunlight.

It's like literally being blind all your life and then suddenly you could see. It's like, wow!

Philippe: Now, you know what I hear in this story is something that I hear consistently among those that I feel -- and this just comes from years and years of hearing great stories and meeting people overcome so much.

I just believe that there are a certain group of people that are chosen to go through certain things, to come out on the other side to help those who may not have a way out, and because there's a reason that you saw that light, there was a reason that you had an "aha" moment because it could have so easily went the other way.

Robert: Oh, absolutely, and I appreciate that point because that was one of the things in seeing that light, as I say, it allowed me to see what you're saying. It's like, "Oh, everything makes sense. Everything is totally perfect."

Philippe: Mm hm.

Robert: And I'm not better than everyone else. I'm not worse than everyone else.

Philippe: Mm hm.

Robert: Yet, we all have the light. We're all enlightened in the sense that the light shines on us all. It's just a question of seeing it -- and it's like when you're alone in the dark, and you're this place where you just can't see anything.

I mean, you have a choice: you can either close your eyes and just go to sleep, or you can look for the light.

Philippe: Mm hm. Mm hm.

Robert: And I think that's what happened for me is I was at the point where I just really lost hope in myself and I tried a lot of things. I had gone through various religions -- I mean, every kind of church and other spirituality and awareness training types of things.

Philippe: Mm hm.

Robert: And psychology, I have a degree in psychology, sociology. I've done the work -- you know, medical, anti-depressants, methadone.

Philippe: Sure.

Robert: All these things I've tried, acupuncture to Zen, A to Z, and it was not until I really let go of everything that I believed and everything I thought I could do for myself and really lost hope.

And it's funny, because you know how there's a saying: "God helps those who help themselves"?

Philippe: Mm hm.

Robert: There's some truth in that, obviously, but He really helps the people who can't help themselves.

Philippe: Mm hmm!

Robert: You know that's the grace.

Philippe: Absolutely.

Robert: When you're hopeless, when you know that you're drowning, like a drowning person, you have to let go to let the person save you.

Philippe: Right. That's right.

Robert: Real salvation is not what a lot of people say, you know, they're saved, whatever.

Philippe: Sure. Sure.

Robert: Just because they say a few magic

words or whatever. It was like "I give up."

Philippe: So, after that, so... did you go through... I think a lot of people remember this in the movie *Ray* when Ray Charles was forced to detox in prison.

Robert: Oh, yeah.

Philippe: Or in jail, from heroin, and was it like that for you? Was it very painful?

Robert: Oh yeah.

Philippe: After seeing that light, and did you see... I mean, was the light before or after that? What was...

Robert: Well, that's a good...

Philippe: That part?

Robert: Yeah, well I went, actually, I'd already gone through a lot of that. I was still really in the middle of that, at that particular time that we're referring to right now. I had gone through a lot of that already, because with heroin addiction, particularly, it's like the worst...

You know, like *Ray* is a good illustration of it. You've probably seen some other kinds of movies where it's like, if you can just imagine the worst flu you've ever had. I mean, that's just the starting point where you're just changing...

Philippe: Mm hm.

Robert: And you're cold, you're hot, you can't eat, you know, you're throwing up. Just everything is just really bad. You'd be feeling like you don't want to be touched, just the sound and touch, and don't even want water. You don't want to take a bath. You smell like death.

Philippe: Mm hm.

Robert: And, yeah, I went through all that, and I just... it took a long time, and then I other illnesses. I had this liver that was really bad, and they said I had this terminal hepatitis C, which can be a deadly disease, which they don't really have a cure for.

You think hospital food is bad, by the way, if you've ever been there. Like jail hospital food, that's like the worst.

Philippe: [Laughter]

Robert: You think you've had a bad year.

Philippe: You know what? I think you're right. It's really, really bad. There's nothing good about it, right?

Robert: No, that's where I was, so I had to go through that, and they took me back...it was like the cells where they have people where they have all these medical problems.

Philippe: Uh huh.

Robert: And when they went back after all this, they did all these blood tests, and they said that it's gone. I was like "What?"

Philippe: Wow!

Robert: So I mean, I've gone, years later and went back, because I've done some crazy things since then. Let me just make sure I've got all these tests that you can take for AIDS and HIV and hepatitis, and all the stuff.

Because that was devastating just to think: "Okay, now not only do I hate myself, but I'm just dying and my life, I can't ever be with anyone because I'll get them sick or whatever," and all that stuff was in my head, and I've gone through what they call an RNA PCR test where they had my blood tested on a molecular level, and the results is zero. I'm like, "Wow!"

Philippe: Wow!

Robert: So that's just grace… grace.

Philippe: This is incredible, so at this point, you are healed, if you will, from heroin, but you're a felon.

Robert: Yeah, that's true.

Philippe: [Laughter]

Robert: And I mean I…

Philippe: [Laughter] I mean, you know, so we kind of trade out a little bit, if you will, for just trying to have a sense of humor here in a very, very heavy topic. So what happens, then? You know, walk us through that "Okay, I am drug-free, but now how do I go on with the rest of my life and what would that look like?"

Robert: Well, my life has been very, very interesting. It's kind of like I compare myself to… do you remember the blind cartoon character named Mr. Magoo?

Philippe: Oh, God, yes.

Robert: Yeah, well it's kind of like that. He's

going to all these different places, and he kind of thinks he knows where he's going, but he's like walking on top of a train or across all these girders, but somehow he gets… you know, something is really taking care of him because he's blind and crossing over these bridges…

Philippe: [Laughter]

Robert: So that's kind of like how my life has gone. I have actually, even with my record, and it's not just one felony. I mean, I've had numerous events of arrest from shoplifting to armed robbery, drug possession for sales and weapons, all kinds of just crazy stuff.

But I was able to get… Yeah, I've done a lot of different things. I've written books. I started because of my credit -- my credit was ruined. As you can imagine, that was the least of my problems.

I mean, when I was trying to build with that, I tried to figure out: "Okay, how do I get this fixed, now? You know, I can't even rent an apartment. I can't even open a savings account because they wouldn't even take my cash.

Philippe: Mm hm.

Robert: They said, "We don't want your money in our bank," and "Get out of here."

Philippe: Well, I think that's fascinating how resourceful you were to figure that out. I mean, I think that's an interview just unto itself.

Robert: Well, that was a whole… yeah, that

was really kind of my claim to fame, as far as writing goes. Because I ended up figuring out how to fix credit back in the 80s, and that was back before you started hearing about credit repair and all that stuff. I was like actually one of the first people that started that whole thing.

Philippe: Wow!

Robert: Because I learned how to do it and I was able to finally clear the stuff, the negative stuff away out of my -- legitimately -- record, so I could at least rent an apartment and then get credit cards, just so I could buy a car and function in society, and so I actually did that.

And I was actually able to also get work. I've worked with some nonprofit agencies. I've worked with rehab facilities. I've worked with the County of Riverside and actually helped create their Alternate Dispute Resolution Program.

I've worked with the Better Business Bureau and Inland Counties Legal Service, Legal Aide, and so I guess, I have something going for me.

Philippe: Absolutely! Absolutely. To find employment and to, like I said, to overcome that to find employment, find housing, after being convicted as a felon and being African-American.

Robert: Yeah, it's not easy. I've even written a book on writing resumes. That's one of my recent things. I worked with the Employment Development Department, actually, for many years. I was the Human Resources consultant.

Yeah, and I worked with CalPERS, the California Public Employees Retirement System, and also as a management trainer and helping the One Stop Career Centers where people are looking for jobs.

Philippe: Mm hm.

Robert: I developed the training I called *Blockbuster Resumes*. So I actually have a book called *Blockbuster Resumes,* if anyone's interested in just how to make your resume so you can really present yourself legitimately, finding how can you overcome those gaps in your history.

Many people just have some gaps or other issues in their work history. I'm sure there are a lot of people out there that really don't have any criminal records that are still having a hard time finding a job, right now.

Philippe: Hell, yeah! [Laughter] I'm sure they are.

Robert: So that's just one of the things. Like I said, I did the credit repair for a while, and so that's kind of how I was able to function. I was just able to fall into these things. I wouldn't say there was no effort on my part. I had to do a lot of research.

Philippe: Now, let me ask you this, Robert. Because I know you as… I know the man, and I know the mission. In chopping that ice that has come up in my mind -- and you tell me if I'm on the right track or not -- and that is "when you were a member of the dark side," if you will.

Robert: Mm hm. [Laughter]

Philippe: Because of your high intellect and high intelligence, there would be an assumption that you were quite good at being bad. Because, you know, drug dealing requires a lot of thought, and there are smart drug dealers and there are dumb drug dealers, and usually the dumb drug dealers end up in prison or dead or both.

And so, it would appear that, praise God, you came out of that and learned the Jedi mind trick and figured it out, but is it true that at one point you were, you know, kind of like a career criminal, and you were really good at what you were doing?

Robert: Well, let's put it this way. There were a lot of things that I did not get caught for doing, but I definitely paid the price for the things that I did, and probably then some.

Philippe: Mm hum.

Robert: I can't say that I was too smart of a criminal, in the sense that I never caught because I have been arrested for the silliest things like shoplifting and for driving around with drugs and guns in my car and getting pulled over for not having my seatbelt on.

And that's just acting all crazy. When you're high on drugs, it's hard to be really a smart criminal, so I'll just put that in the statement.

Philippe: No, I'll hold that, that's good. That's

good.

Robert: So, yeah, I mean there were a lot of things that I ended up doing, I would say, probably, on the intellectual end of it. I got involved in alternate identities and creating new identities for people, and things like that.

Philippe: Mm hm. Mm hm.

Robert: And I'm not proud of this. I'm just saying those are some things that a lot of people didn't know how to do or whatever -- but, a lot of it happened just because I knew a little bit about the system.

Philippe: Sure.

Robert: Credit and stuff, but as I said, I got in trouble for most of the things that I did, and I think I've gotten… I've suffered for the things that I did that allowed me to really try to get back and make up for that.

Philippe: Yeah.

Robert: And that's why I've written books, and I've done a lot of consulting. I've consulted with hundreds of individuals.

Philippe: Absolutely.

Robert: I've consulted with people about turning their lives around, or recouping their financial things, about career types of things, and about writing. Again, I keep doing my writing.

Philippe: You were pretty much set, saying that, "Okay, yep, here is my pass. I've been there and done that. Not going through that again," and you pretty much trying to set you life up saying, "Okay, I'm just going to live under the umbrella of being a felon, but I'm not going to live like a felon."

Robert: Yeah, absolutely.

Philippe: Is that kind of accurate? And then all of a sudden, you know, here we come to Easter Sunday, 2013, and you get a call or email? Or what happened? How does that happen?

Robert: I got the phone call, actually, on Good Friday. You know that April Friday night.

Philippe: So, it definitely was a Good Friday.

Robert: Yeah, it was definitely a very Good Friday.

Philippe: [Laughter]

Robert: And, it had been many, many years since the last thing that I'd gotten in trouble for.

Philippe: Yeah, how long was that part? How long was it before the pardon?

Robert: It was 1996.

Philippe: Okay, so it took quite a bit of time, okay.

Robert: Yeah. Yeah, it was quite a bit of time, and I had, you know, since then, I've been like clean and sober, since actually… well, since when I was arrested. But I was still out on bail, so I was doing a lot of stuff up to the final day, which was actually October 30th.

Philippe: Mm hm.

Robert: October 31st of 1997, that's what I call

my "re-birth day" because that was the day I went to jail.

Philippe: Mm hm.

Robert: That makes my final sentence for the last time. Like I said, these are some things that had reoccurred over time. It wasn't like I just got in trouble one time and saw the light, and "Okay, now everything is perfect." No.

Philippe: Um hm.

Robert: It was not even close, so I really want to encourage anyone who's had trouble, especially something that…

Philippe: Absolutely. Absolutely.

Robert: You know, just like you said, it's not about living and thinking about my past all the time. It's really about living in the present, because when I say, "I've seen the light," that is not just an intellectual exercise or just a belief system. It's really a present-moment experience.

Philippe: Mm hm.

Robert: Right here. Right now. It's really the only time that really matters. What do I say, today? Who do I want to be, today?

Philippe: Sure.

Robert: You know, I'm going to try to live my life in sort of one day at a time, even though I do make plans, and I mean I do learn from my past mistakes, so it's not like you just pretend it never happened, or you just don't have any idea what you're going to do the next day.

But I really try to put the major focus on, "Okay, who do I want to be today," and really turning the positive around and not just positive thinking, but really looking at positive kind of questions.

Philippe: Mm hm.

Robert: One of my questions that I like to ask a lot is: What's the best thing that could happen?

Philippe: Mm hm. Mm hm. And I like that. I like that a lot.

Robert: Yeah, what's the best thing that could happen? And that's on a general idea or in a specific situation, rather than thinking: "Okay. Well, the worst thing that can happen is I'll do this, and I won't get the job," or whatever. What's the best thing that can happen? Hey, what if they give you a better job than you even applied for?

Philippe: Sure.

Robert: What if you sell your life story and make this giant movie and all these things, whatever it is you're trying to do?

Philippe: Now, what's really cool is that you're also like a professor. Do you teach, at the collegiate level, screenwriting?

Robert: I do. I teach the screenwriting and then creative writing. I have a couple of colleges that I teach at, and I've been like a visiting lecturer at a couple of colleges, and I went over to Bahrain in the Middle East.

Philippe: Wow!

Robert: You know, a year and a half ago, and taught the class to military students over there and we talked about the hero's journey.

Philippe: Sure.

Robert: A metaphor for what we all go through. We start in one place, something happens and then we end up learning these lessons along the way.

Philippe: Right. Right.

Robert: And we get the end stories, or we have allies and we have enemies, and sometimes we get betrayed and sometimes we end up where all seems lost.

But there are those lessons that you learn, and whether it's in, like you talked about here, you had some early losses in your life.

Philippe: Mm hm.

Robert: Your mother's passing and those are tragedies, and they're difficulties, and they're painful -- or dealing with poverty -- but in a sense, the good side of that is you make some commitments to not go into drugs and crime and gangs.

Philippe: Mm hm.

Robert: And so, we almost don't want to say, "Well, because that happened, that's why I'm this way."

Philippe: Mm hm.

Robert: But it's like without the crucifixion, there's no resurrection.

Philippe: Mm hm. Mm hm. That is so, so true. I would assume that your story, your life, rather, has helped you tremendously in your creative work in screenwriting and writing books.

Robert: Oh, it has. I mean, I've written books, a lot of them out of my experience like *The Light,* of course, was almost like a memoir, originally. It was almost like writing out my -- what they call like a fifth step or confessional -- just to get some stuff out of my system. It's like a therapeutic process.

Philippe: Mm hm. Mm hm.

Robert: And I kind of teach that in creative writing, and you can be a therapist for yourself, but also you can help other people because you know things that other people don't know.

I was a spokesperson for Capital One for a while because I know about identity theft. You know, I had a lot of different reasons how I know about it, but I wrote a book called *Identity Theft* years ago, and I helped a lot of people solve their problems.

Here, if you've got this crime that's occurred to you -- identity theft -- here's some things you can do to protect yourself, or things you can do to resolve that issue. So I've taken negative situations -- you know like I've worked in rehabilitation centers.

I've worked helping people get jobs, and yeah, I was like the worst employee in the world, at times -- you know, so I mean, I know what it's like to be the guy that will hear: "How can we fire this guy?"

Philippe: Mm hm.

Robert: Why did he hire us in the first place? Or, where is he? You know, [laughter] he's supposed to be at his desk, and I haven't seen him for two weeks, and he won't answer this phone, or he's like nodding out at his desk, or he's drunk or he's, you know, "that" employee.

Or like, "What happened to that computer that was supposed to be sitting here?" [Laughter] You know, anyway.

Philippe: [Laughter]

Robert: So, here comes the worst employee in the universe, to becoming a Human Resources Consultant with the California State Employment Development Department.

Philippe: Wow.

Robert: You know, teaching people and managers -- managers was one of my jobs, years ago, management consulting, showing here's how you hire the right people. Here's how you work with people who have these issues.

Philippe: Mm hm.

Robert: I mean, obviously, you don't necessarily want to hire somebody who can't really do the job or who can't function. Yeah, you do have to learn how to deal with some issues, these problems.

You know, there are ways you can work with them. And people who have the worst scenarios, they can, and they have turned around. So it's helped me see things differently.

I was being really non-judgmental. You know, you see -- yeah, you live in the Bay area. You go to certain areas, say, in Oakland or in San Francisco in some places, you've got all these homeless people lying on the streets.

Philippe: Sure. Sure.

Robert: I mean, you want to cross the street, or step over people like, let's say, like in the Tenderloin, and some of these districts in certain areas, but I was one of those people.

Philippe: Wow!

Robert: And I know that there's a light and that I talk about the light a lot, but it's like everybody is enlightened. You know, the light is in everyone.

Philippe: Mm hm.

Robert: No matter what your poverty level, no matter what your politics, or your nationality or your race, or what your lifestyle or your choices that you make -- there's still a light within you.

Philippe: Absolutely.

Robert: And so, if I try to see that, and I can -- you know, it's not always easy to see it because it's hard enough to see it in yourself, but if you don't see it in yourself, you can't really see it in anyone else.

And if I know I've been forgiven for all this stuff, and I was like that, and today, I'm not like the perfect person, but you wouldn't recognize me.

Philippe: Sure.

Robert: If you saw the before and after, I know that it's possible for one.

Philippe: What an amazing before and after. So, here you are now afterward, and you have all of these books. Where did the idea come from to do a biopic on Cecil B. DeMille? I mean that was huge!

Robert: Yeah, that was what I was saying before, you kind of called me "the DeMille guy," you know, Cecil, giving him his close-up.

Philippe: Yeah.

Robert: Giving him his close-up, and people who've seen Sunset Boulevard, for example, you see him as the guy: "I'm ready for my close-up, Mr. DeMille." You know, the big king -- Samson and Delilah, you know, these big blockbuster movies like "The Greatest Show on Earth."

That's Cecil B. DeMille, really the biggest director, kind of man who had been in Hollywood. He was out here 100 years ago, in 1913, when this was just orange groves and desert. California, and people were like "Why would anyone want to go out there?"

And making movies, in people's minds, was just like... you know, they became like a little peep show, when you say the word "movies" you're looking at a five-cent nickelodeon where you turn a crank, and you see a stripper or a mountain lion or something for five seconds.

Philippe: [Laughter] Right.

Robert: So, when I studied him -- I actually went back to school, after all the stuff I had gone through in the past -- and I got my undergraduate degree in sociology, and psychology, and I actually went to law school for a while.

I was going to be an attorney. Then deciding, no, I really want to do writing. I really want to get back to kind of my love of what I'd wanted to do when I was really a little kid.

Philippe: Mm hm.

Robert: That was something that I always liked -- movies and I liked writing, and it was, "Here, I really would want to be a writer. That way I can live all these lives, and be all these people through writing stories.

So anyway, I went back to graduate school, eventually, and got a Master of Fine Arts in creative writing, and part of that was -- screenwriting was my emphasis -- so a lot of it was about film history, and theory, and so when I studied that, I really learned about Cecile B. DeMille.

Really, how undervalued he was, as far as "Wow, this guy, he's really basically created this industry, the film-making, the movie-making in

Hollywood."

Philippe: Mm hm.

Robert: DeMille was the one who really put Hollywood on the map; Paramount Studios was just started out of a little horse barn that he had rented.

Philippe: Um hm.

Robert: He used to do those silent movies and now it's a big, giant industry, and I just thought, "Wow! His own life was really amazing," and then it was like these contradictions. Like on one hand, here he wants to do *The Ten Commandments,* all these biblical epics, but here he's got mistresses, and he's treating people badly, and he's saying, "I'm going to steal the plant that I need for the movie, so I can put it in the crown of thorns for Jesus. [Laughter]

Philippe: So, you're talking about leading a double-life, huh?

Robert: Exactly, so I just thought he was so fascinating, because not only did I just enjoy the movies, you know, they were just big and fun, if you've seen like *The Ten Commandments, The Greatest Show on Earth,* you know, Charlton Heston and Yule Brynner, and all these guys. I thought, well his life was not like, I would say, like mine, because he wasn't a criminal.

Philippe: Mm hm.

Robert: But he had some down places. I mean he lost everything at one point -- I mean, his wife, and his daughter, family, they left him. Because he was philandering, he was doing all these wild things, and he treated people kind of badly because he was such a tyrant, and then he saw the light.

So he had this turn around moment, and so when I really learned about his personal story and his real, internal story; he came from a single family home. His father died when he was 10 and his mother struggled to raise him and his brother, and his brother was actually a lot smarter than he was.

And so, he just had a vision, and he was just somebody who I really had learned to come to admire, and I thought, "Wow! What if there was a movie about his life? That would really be a great movie." You know, just like *The Aviator* or A *Beautiful Mind*.

Philippe: Mm hm.

Robert: You know, even movies like Great Gatsby, you know, and that's kind of a spectacular story.

Philippe: Sure. Sure.

Robert: I was like, "Wow!"

Philippe: Incredible.

Robert: So that's what's what I'm doing now. We're in the process, going through development. You know I've written the novel, called *C.B. DeMille: The Man Who Invented Hollywood*. We have the Web site, CBDeMille.com, by the way, if anyone wants to see a little bit more about the movie, CBDeMille.com really goes into more details.

Philippe: Yeah, I was going to say. Well, how can people get in contact with you? What is -- I'm sure you have more than one Web site -- you know, what are they?

Robert: Oh, sure.

Philippe: What's the main ones?

Robert: Yeah, the CBDeMille.com is more like for the movie, and you can contact me there, but I'm on Twitter as @RobertHammond.

You can actually find the books that we were talking about, *The Light*. You can actually get like a free sample the first chapter of it at NewWayPress.com.

So, it's NewWayPress.com that's the publisher that has that and you can find me there. I'm also on LinkedIn, and Facebook and places like that.

I have another little Web site, as RobertHammond.tumblr.com, which is that type of blog, and I've a lot of information there, too.

Philippe: Excellent! Excellent for this, and that is your journey began because you went through, you know, a pretty horrific identity crisis, I think, that was racially motivated, and nothing you could really do about it, so kind of forced into a situation that you didn't ask to be in.

So, we all understand that, when we go through multiple identity crisis or crises. What have you been able to do, and do differently, where that level of stress that could happen with an identity crisis -- or in your future getting ready to become a Hollywood type, if you will, that you won't end up in some of those same situations and circles?

Robert: Oh, those are excellent questions. Yeah because, you know, so many people do sometimes slip and fall into traps. They kind of get full of themselves, and I think that's been one of my problems before with the identity, as I have gotten wrapped up in not really knowing who I was, and trying to be something that I wasn't.

I'll give you really three quick steps. I would say for personal transformation, I believe that work for everyone.

Philippe: Mm hm.

Robert: I believe it worked for me, and it's not about religion or certain belief systems or anything. But, if just do these three things that I'll just go over real quickly, your life will never be the same. The first step to that true peace inside is to stand still in the light.

Philippe: Mmm!

Robert: In other words, just stand still, be still and know in the light. You know, let that light shine in your life, and find it within yourself. That's step one.

Number two is to believe in the light. So in other words, the light itself is this revelation of the truth that if you are really still long enough to really watch, you'll see yourself more clearly, and you'll see what life is about.

You'll kind of awaken to this -- and this is all a process, and not just a formula that I'm giving here, that you may start believing that what you're seeing, and that's where the faith is developed.

Even just that little faith, like a little mustard seed. If you have that little bit of faith -- like you're open and willing to be open and willing -- you can move mountains. You know, your whole life can change.

Philippe: Absolutely.

Robert: And then, ultimately, it's walking in the light, and so that's kind of where you're believing and trusting and living kind of a life of faith, and not just a religious ritual or anything, but just daily, moment by moment, living in really in the presence -- you know, I say the presence of God, that's my experience.

Philippe: Mm hm.

Robert: It is walking in the light, you know, it is a way that really transcends religion. It transcends belief systems, transcends rituals, and if we keep doing that, no matter what our situation is.

Because we'll have what seem to be "ups" and seem to be "downs." We'll have different kinds of situations coming into our lives, if we continue, back to that story I said before, it's like you're running around looking for your keys or your glasses, but you have them with you all the time.

Philippe: Mm hm.

Robert: You know, everybody's enlightened.

Philippe: Mm hm.

Robert: And it's like once you see that within in yourself, you really see this more and more, and it's just not a one-time event and then, "Okay, now, I'm on top of the mountain, here."

Philippe: Right. Right.

Robert: That's it, and it's like giving up service, and you asked, what's in the future? I mean, I teach classes. I try to help, when I can. I do some consulting, writing, and probably another book.

Actually, I've just come out with *Finding the Light Within,* and you can find that one on Amazon because it just came out. Just search for *Finding the Light Within* by Robert Hammond.

Philippe: Mm hm.

Robert: But, the light, the one we were talking about before, is really just a way of seeing. I think people who read that book *The Light* will see not just my story, and say, "Oh, wow! You went through all this stuff, and how you came out," but really learn some lessons.

Because that's what I tried to do with it, is really shine light and give people ways that they can identify, because most people who read it, they actually say they identify with the character.

Because everyone's going to feel a little bit out

of place at times, or they feel like they've gone too far and can't get back, and like they're searching for something -- they don't really know what it is, and where it is.

Philippe: Mm hm.

Robert: But they join all these different groups, trying to look for answers or take whatever they take and get lost sometimes.

Philippe: Robert, you are one of my heroes. Your story completely resonates with me, and you are "a light" that shines very, very bright, and I think you're going to help thousands and thousands, if not millions of people who have gone through what you have or worse, but the world is much better that you showed up. That's for sure.

Robert: Thank you so much, Philippe. I can tell you the same thing for you. You're also a light. I appreciate your light shining, and giving me an opportunity to be here with you, today.

Philippe: Absolutely! And then, this is not the end because I want you back on the show, so [laughter] you want to make a commitment! [Laughter]

Robert: Oh, I will, absolutely! I've enjoyed this time, and definitely look forward to doing some time with you again.

Philippe: And I so appreciate you. Thank you so much, and let's talk again soon.

Robert: Take care.

The Return: A Writer Gives Back

WGN Radio: Nick Digilio Interview with Author Robert Hammond

Nick Digilio: Nick Digilio here, on The Voice of Chicago 720 WGN. We're live in the all-state studio of the seventh floor of the Trib Tower. I'm filling in for Bill Leff and I'll be filling in for Bill Leff all of next week, as well. So, in that, that's going to be fun.

So, facebook.com/nickdshow is the best way to stay connected to us. You can also send your text anytime to 24720. My first guest tonight is a pretty fascinating story himself, as well as being the author of several books including *Ready When You Are - Cecil B. DeMille's Ten Commandments for Success*.

And so we're going to talk about Cecil B. DeMille, but also talk about our guest's personal life, which has really, he did a complete 180 and changed his life, and we'll talk a little bit about that. My guest is Robert Hammond. Robert, welcome to the show.

Robert Hammond: Hey Nick, thanks for having me on.

Nick: Absolutely. Let's talk a little bit, before we get to Cecil B. DeMille and the book about Cecil B. DeMille, let's talk a little bit about what happened to you. I mean, you turned your life around. You know, you were in and out of jail and rehab and stuff like that. Tell me a little bit about how you changed your life.

Robert: I did, yeah. Well, it's a long story, but the bottom line of it is that, I was at the end of my rope. I kind of compare myself to, you ever seen, like a dead dog lying on the road, there was nothing left, and I saw the light. And I mean, and I say that in the literal sense. Not just a religious belief system or anything else, but it was, I got to, I guess maybe a near death experience, and I had this awakening that really let me see things very, very differently.

And that was quite some time back. It's been, well, originally that happened back in the late 80's, that experience. I had a little trouble processing it all, so it's been actually, I think 1997 when I finally just kind of cleared everything out of my system so to speak, with the whole, the drugs. I was on heroin and cocaine and everything.

I was in prison, my life was over basically, and things have changed. Since then, I've gone back and went and got a Masters in Fine Arts degree, I'm a college professor right now, teach creative writing, screen writing, movie producer, screen writer, author, numerous books, and things have changed.

Nick: It's amazing. Now, do you speak to people and you do some consulting, do you not?

Robert: I do, yeah. I have a consulting company, Robert Hammond Consulting, if you want to look that up. It mostly focuses on creative writing, because what I found is one of the issues for me, and I think a lot of people, is that we have this untold story in ourselves. And I think it was Maya Angelou who says something along the lines of "There's no greater agony than bearing an untold story inside you."

And so my consulting right now is focused mostly, I deal with some people in recovery, and I do talk to people about that. I write articles and blogs and I've written about a dozen books on different topics. *Ready When You Are,* actually, is about turning your life around, and I use the metaphor of making movies, Cecil B. DeMille and we'll get into that.

Nick: Yeah.

Robert: I'm sure, later.

Nick: Yeah.

Robert: My website is where I do consulting.

It's mostly writing, creative writing, and helping people. you know everyone has got a story to tell, and whether you're just, say, a business person and you wanted to say, "Here, I wanted to show people how to make money, or I want to show them how to retire whatever your personal business is." Or you have your life, story, which I've told in different ways. If you go to any of these, if you're familiar with these, the Twelve Steps program people—

Nick: Sure.

Robert: —that's what they do, they tell their story and that's part of the healing. So, that's what I help people get that story out and get it in writing and get the books published. Or to write screenplays and adapt their stories to film and television.

Nick: Now, before all the trouble began and the downward spiral happened in your life, were you into film, or were you into writing? Was it something that you had pursued when you were younger before all the bad stuff happened?

Robert: I was, and it was kind of, you know I had one of those, I guess, identity crisis part of my life story and actually I tell that story in a novel. I actually ended up novelizing it. It was originally a memoir, but it's a novel called *The Light*, which you and me will talk about that a little bit later. But yeah, I started out, when I was very young. I mean, I was a voracious reader, I mean, I loved movies, I loved to write.

I always had that emotionally sensitivity, I guess you could call it. So I could write poetry, I was kind of a weird, kind of a loner kid. I was African-American, but even though we grew up in Washington D.C. for a while, we ended up moving out. My father's a military and he's actually a medical doctor, we moved around so much. I always ended up kind of like being out of place, at times I would be the only black kid in the whole white school.

Nick: Yeah.

Robert: So I just didn't feel comfortable, so I always tried to make up for that, one way or the other. Whether it's retreating in myself or just kind of being the class clown, or acting out, or whatever. But yeah, I did a lot of writing when I was younger, wrote a lot of poetry and letters, and some short stories.

And it wasn't until years later though, even while I was in the middle of all my problems, which I ended up getting into, the drugs and sex rock and roll lifestyle. I was in Hollywood, I was writing in, writing books and I was even doing radio interviews like this, and I would be strung out on heroin, I mean, I would literally be talking to a guy like yourself.

Nick: Yeah.

Robert: Yeah, quite a while back and I would be shooting up, I was doing that, it was crazy.

Nick: Yeah, jeez.

Robert: It was terrible.

Nick: So, but you did have that creative bug before all the bad stuff happened. You know, it's interesting, when you wrote this novel, but like you said, it started out as a memoir, but when it ended up as a novel, was it really a cathartic thing for you to write this? Was it a big deal for you to write it?

Robert: Absolutely, yeah. It was one of, I think, the biggest things that's really kept me clean and sober and kind of halfway sane, was really just getting this story out of my system, because it allowed me, it's like a therapy. It's like when a person goes through a psychiatrist, or a therapist, you are just talking, basically.

You're telling them all these big things that you can't really tell anyone, and so writing, and even people who are in these recovery programs, Twelve Steps, that's part of it is you write out this personal inventory. Kind of, your resentments, your fears, your guilts and stuff that might just be holding people back. And everybody's story is different, I mean, it's not like everybody's had, even in my own case, I didn't come from an abused childhood. My father was a doctor, my mother's got a Master's in Social Work, we're relatively well off, military family, and—

Nick: Yeah.

Robert: —medical, but you still have these,

everybody's got some kind of trauma. Whether it's, like, someone who's actually been abused physically, sexually, emotionally, or they just felt totally lost and alienated, misunderstood or whatever it is. So these things, dark stories, I think we all have inside of us, and that was a big part of my recovery and my enlightenment.

It's really a spiritual path, from my perspective, to get those stories out, tell my story, and share with others. And you also connect with people because you find out, well, I felt the same way, even though my life might be very different, you find that people do have more in common than we think.

Nick: Yeah. And the book is called *The Light* and you can get that probably on the internet. Is it available, like if people go to Amazon, or the internet or anything like that?

Robert: Yeah, you can get it, The Light, by Robert Hammond, you can get on Amazon and Barnes & Noble, and probably your local bookstore should have it as well.

Nick: Okay.

Robert: My website again, Robert Hammond Consulting.

Nick: Roberthammondconsulting.com is also there. Before, we're taking a quick break, Robert, but I want to know what drew you to Cecil B. DeMille, before we start talking about the book.

Robert: Okay.

Nick: Was it, did he have a similar, did he have a similar epiphany as well?

Robert: Well, the difference, yeah, he definitely did. Definitely not like mine, he was not a drug addict—

Nick: Right, right.

Robert: —or a criminal, like I was. I was Robert, the thief. DeMille was a man who had a lot of contradictions, and he grew up in a strict home but it was a single parent family and he had this vision of doing his big things. No one really supported him, except for a very small couple of guys that he worked with, when he came out. And so, what drew me to him was when I finally went back to school, I actually went to law school for a while.

And then I decided what I really wanted to get back to my writing I went back to get a Master of Fine Arts, and that's where I studied Film History, and I learned about DeMille. And his story was so amazing because of this vision, and the spade that he had in, plus the contradictions.

Because on one hand he was doing *Ten Commandments* and all these biblical epics. On the other hand, he's going through this infidelity and kind of a tyrant on the set, so he's not living the bible lifestyle that fits with his movies.

Nick: Yeah, okay, Robert, hang on. Fascinating character that was Cecil B. DeMille, obviously one of the, one of the biggest contributors to the history of Hollywood and cinema, was Cecil B DeMille. And the book is called *Ready When You Are - Cecil B. DeMille's Ten Commandments for Success,* we'll talk about that. Also, Robert Hammond's book, The Light, is also available. Roberthammondconsulting.com is the website, when we come back, we'll talk more about Cecil B. DeMille, Hollywood's coolest founding father.

You have questions or comments or if you're a DeMille fan, it's 312-981-7200, 312-981-7200. Facebook.com/nickdshow, and you can send your texts anytime you want to 24720. More with my guest Robert Hammond, author of *Ready When You Are - Cecil B DeMille's Ten Commandments for Success,* coming up, after this on WGN.

Nick Digilio here, on The Voice of Chicago 720 WGN. We are live in the all-state studio on the seventh floor of the Tribune Tower. Here until 06:00 am, I'm keeping you company all night long. Bill Leff will be in at 10:00 am, and he'll be taking a vacation next week, so I will be filling in this time slot all week next week, as well.

And as well as manning my shows on Friday nights and Saturday nights. So, you can get all the information at wgnradio.com. You can also check us out at facebook.com/nickdshow. My guest right now is Robert Hammond, he's the author of several books, including a novel called *The Light,* which is based on his true, his real story.

We're about to talk about this book called

Ready When You Are - Cecil B. DeMille's Ten Commandments for Success. So Robert, tell me about the origin of this book, how you started on it, and what made you, what inspired you to write a book about Cecil B. DeMille.

Robert: Okay, yeah, very good. Cecil B. DeMille, as I mentioned, I started studying when I was, went back for a Master in Fine Arts in Creative Writing, and I studied film history, and I was surprised, they covered so many different great directors, and when I found out about DeMille, his whole thing was in a 700 page film history, he had about, like, two paragraphs.

Nick: No, really?

Robert: I was like, wait a minute. Now, I know this guy has done more than what you're saying here, so I just did my own research and I ended up writing one of my papers on him, and actually did, my Master's thesis became a screen play based on his life. If you've ever seen movies like *The Aviator*, about Howard Hughes.

Nick: Sure.

Robert: Or *A Beautiful Mind*, or *Ray*, those types of biopic stories. That's how I got really fascinated with Cecil B. DeMille was actually when I researched his life. Especially the whole, the biblical epics. To me that was an interesting concept. With *The Passion of The Christ* had been out, and that was a major, a big movie that people were controversial about, saying, "No one wants to see that kind of a movie," but it became a big blockbuster.

Nick: Yeah, yeah.

Robert: And DeMille was the same kind of guy, he was like, I want to tell these big stories and the producers, you know he's the creative guy, Mr. DeMille, and the producers, the people with the money, they're like, "Well, no, nobody wants to see a bunch of old guys in beards and table cloths running around the desert."

And that's what they were saying about the *Ten Commandments,* which most people have seen. And it still comes on every year, around Easter or Passover, with Charlton Heston, Yul Brynner, and this is a movie made back in the 50's. And so there's something to those big stories, and when I learned his life and realized his life was bigger than life too. Not quite like Moses, or Jesus—

Nick: Yeah.

Robert: —that he told movies about, but he was a bigger than life guy. I mean he made 70 big movies out here. DeMille came to California 100 years ago, 1913. 100 years ago and this is orange groves and desert. So anyone even talking about going to California for any kind of business, they were out of their mind. And so it was kind of like when Bugsy Siegel came out and built Las Vegas.

Nick: Yeah.

Robert: A desert, and he envisioned all these casinos. Kind of like that in a sense, that he was able to see things that no one else could see. So that was one of my fascinations and that's when I wrote *Ready When You Are,* I took his personal story and then I blended it in with more of a self-help book. These are some ideas that if we took these and lived our lives like that, which is, one of the things that's changed my life.

Living a life of vision, being visionary, humility, these are some basic principles that, in spite of some of his outlandishness, I found some very humbling aspects of his, of who he was. Because he really did treat other people badly in some ways, but in other ways he was one of the most generous people out there.

He really elevated women, and minorities, and he's brought a lot of people into this business and he really respected the creation and animals, all kinds of things that is very surprising. He was a very sensitive person. Well…

Nick: Yeah. You know, we hear more, those things, those attributes that you just described don't normally come to mind when you first hear the name Cecil B. DeMille. Because when you hear Cecil B. DeMille, first you think big, you know? That's like the first thing that I think of—

Robert: Right.

Nick: —when I hear Cecil B. DeMille, is really big, really lavish, very long and just, Hollywood with a capital H, is the first—

Robert: Exactly.

Nick: —thing that I think of when I think of Cecil B DeMille. And then, the second thing I think of are the things that I've heard about his character over the course of many years, and that he was in fact over. He was over the top, he was a bit of a tyrant, what he wanted is what he had to get, and things like that. But all the nice attributes that you just described, you don't normally hear combined with Cecil B. DeMille, so I think one of the reasons why you probably obviously wrote this book.

Robert: It is, yeah, and again, because I'm a person of contradictions as was discussed a little bit. On the one hand, yeah, I come from this really great family, and upper middle class, but then I ended up in the ghetto. Ended up in jail, ended up homeless, end up in drugs and just totally insane. When people who come from really bad backgrounds and they do very, very well—

Nick: Yeah.

Robert: —and they just struggle a different way. But at the same end there's a part of me just says I think within everyone that doesn't always do what you think is the best thing. In my case it went a little too far, because I don't think the average person ends up ever in jail, or being a heroin addict. I used to carry a gun, I was an armed robber, I was a drug dealer, I mean all the craziest—

Nick: Yeah.

Robert: —things out there that you could do, I was doing them. I'm just lucky that I'm me in my life today.

Nick: What are, very briefly because we've only got a couple of minutes, what are, if you can give me the *Cliffs Notes* version, what are the *Ten Commandments for Success* that Cecil B. DeMille…

Robert: Well, let me just go over a couple of them really quick. The biggest one that I thought was very contradictory was point number one, be visionary. I mean, we know that if you can really start seeing something that's bigger than everyone else, your life will be different.

The other one was being humble. He was a very big person, very arrogant in a lot of ways, very demanding, but at the same end he had a certain humility because he knew that there was something greater than himself. And that was his, that spiritual element, and that's why he, he actually, the spiritual wakening he ended up having was what led him to do those biblical epics.

Nick: Yeah.

Robert: He started realizing, that this lifestyle, and all the decadence of Hollywood, and all the stuff I'm going through with my family, I'm losing, I don't want to lose my wife, and my daughter and everything else, and so, it was about also. One of the other ones, be courageous.

So again, there are ten commandments, each

one of them is a very strong principle and it's based on personal stories that we talk about, about DeMille. People who read the book, they've said that it's really changed their lives. People break down in tears because they see some of the family things that we all go through.

Nick: Yeah.

Robert: The courageousness. And being spectacular, you mentioned that about him, that's one of his commandments, just really go out there, and do it up.

Nick: Yeah.

Robert: So that's kind of what I've tried to do with my life and that's I think, he's been an influence to me. I went back and got my Masters in Fine Arts and now I teach creative writing and I write books and novels and screenplays. And we're actually making a movie about his life now, that's my biggest project, Cecil B. DeMille biopic.

Nick: Well, that's great, that's great. Well, that's great. The book is called *Ready When You Are - Cecil B. DeMille's Ten Commandments for Success,* and there are also other things that Robert has written, including *The Light.* You can go to roberthammondconsulting.com for further information. And there's actually a website if you want to learn more about Cecil B. DeMille, cecilbdemille.com, are his…

Robert: There is a cecilbdemille.com website which is very good and I've actually met his granddaughter, who runs that one.

Nick: Okay.

Robert: CBDemille.com is my website, which actually gets into his life and would be... so a couple of different ones.

Nick: Okay. RobertHammondConsulting.com and CBDemille.com, the book is called *Ready When You Are - Cecil B. DeMille's Ten Commandments for Success*. Well, congratulations on the turnaround in your life, Robert. That's really inspiring and really great, and I wish you best success.

Robert: Thank you so much.

Nick: Alright.

Robert: Have a great one.

Nick: Alright, take care.

Robert: Take care.

Nick: Robert Hammond, everybody. A great true story right there about a guy who spiraled down to the absolute bottom and clawed his way back up and is now an author, a successful writer, a professor and his book is called *Ready When You Are - Cecil B. DeMille's Ten Commandments for Success,* in which he found inspiration in the life and the story of Cecil B. DeMille.

Really, really interesting, very cool stuff.

A Distant Memory: Revisited

The scarlet thread now wraps itself around my neck like an umbilical cord. I am drowning in an amniotic sea of Primordial Death. Panic pours out like water, my bones are out of joint. The cords of death entangle me; the torrents of destruction overwhelm me. The cords of the grave coil around me; the snares of death confront me.

My God, My God, why hast Thou forsaken me? Why are you so far from saving me, so far from the words of my groaning? You brought me out of the womb and made me trust in you even at my mother's breast. From birth I was cast upon you, from my mother's womb you have been my God. Do not be far from me, for trouble is near and there is no help.

The Three Assassins stalk me. Surround me. Like roaring lions tearing their prey, they open their mouths wide against me, engulfing me. I am lost in the Abyss.

Suddenly I awaken. Sweating, screaming, gasping for breath. The sheets are wrapped around my neck like a hangman's noose as the nightmare fades into the nothingness from whence it came.

Beyond the Hero's Journey: 7 Steps to Transformation

The hero's journey is a deep level of storytelling that connects us all at the core of who we are and what we are capable of becoming. There are many versions of the underlying stages and many heroes that follow this path, from ancient saviors like Moses and Jesus to modern literary characters including Alice in Wonderland, Superman, and Harry Potter.

In some ways, we all travel a hero's journey from birth to death and beyond. Look at your own life and see how you have followed a similar path. Where are you now along the journey?

Think about how the hero's journey applies to your story and the book you are writing. Here is my version of the hero's journey, going a little further using seven steps to transformation:

1. **Conception** – Every story has a beginning. In the beginning was the Word, and the Word was with God, and the Word was God. The

Word is also illustrated as the seed and the light. Many heroes' journey stories begin with a supernatural or unusual birth. Moses was sent down the Nile River in a basket and was raised in the Pharaoh's household. Jesus was born in an immaculate conception to the Virgin Mary through the Holy Spirit. In modern stories we see how Superman was sent to Earth as a child from the planet Krypton by his father just before it was destroyed. Harry Potter was born with a special birthmark on his forehead and raised with relatives. In my novel, *The Light,* I begin with birth narrative that ties in to the story's theme of rebirth and renewal.

Every story has an origin as well. The seed may come to you as a flash of inspiration or an idea. The conception of *Transformed by Writing* occurred while I was going through Christine Kloser's *Transformational Authors Experience.* Having already written more than a dozen books, including the recent publication of my novel, *The Light,* I thought I was ready to take a break from writing for a while. As I began listening in on the calls from various experts on every topic from personal transformation to publishing, promoting, and internet marketing, I realized that there was an unfilled need for a book about transformational writing, with an emphasis on the healing power of stories. I knew that my experience was unique and that many people had asked for advice over the years about how to write their books and become published authors. Hence, an idea was conceived.

Sometimes a story can be conceived by the use of deliberate writing prompts. My friend, Rhonda Gould Smolarek once posed the following prompt in her writing blog: *Imagine yourself waking up blindfolded and tied to a chair.* Based on that "what if" scenario, I developed several stories and even included it in the opening of *The Light* as well as in the screenplay for *Destiny's Lance,* about a graduate student's search for the legendary spear of destiny.

What if you woke up blindfolded and tied to a chair? What if someone you knew was the one tied to the chair and it was up to you to save them? What if your story holds the only key to saving someone's life and setting them free?

2. Root – As in the Parable of the Sower, the seed may land along the wayside or on stony ground where it is eaten by birds before it takes root. The seed may land among thorns and thistles where it is strangled by temptations and the cares of this world before it comes to light. Moses was raised in

Pharaoh's court where he lived a life of luxury and power. He later led the children of Israel through the wilderness and through the Red Sea. Satan tempted Jesus in the wilderness with the riches of this world before Jesus began his official ministry. Every hero goes through a period of developing their roots as they connect to the deeper purpose.

This book began to take root as I began brainstorming titles and concepts as part my book roadmap process. Roots develop as the project begins to take shape and grow on its own. How has your story taken root?

3. **Calling** – The idea of a "calling" has often been used to describe what is really more of a direct order or mission. When Moses went up to Mount Sinai to encounter the burning bush, he was given a command to bring his people out of bondage in Egypt. The prophet Jonah was called by God to go to Nineva and tell the people to change their ways or they would be destroyed. In *Star Wars,* Luke Skywalker receives a call for help from Princess Leia. Harry Potter receives an invitation to wizard school. Sometimes the calling is from the still, small, voice within…gently guiding us to the Light. What's your calling?

4. **Baptism** – Also known as the initiation or immersion process, Moses experienced his baptism into the ways of his mission on the backside of the desert. Jonah, having resisted the calling to preach to the people of Ninevah was cast overboard from a ship and ended up being swallowed by a great fish (belly of the whale). Jesus went through the baptism of John in the River Jordan but foretold of coming baptism by fire that all who truly sought to follow him would eventually experience.

   Whenever I get deeply into a new book or film project, I immerse myself in the subject matter. Ask anyone who knows me what I think about Cecil B. DeMille for example. Once I realized I was going to write the biopic about the greatest showman on Earth, I totally immersed myself into everything related to DeMille by reading every book about his life and watching every movie that he made. I joined the Hollywood Heritage Foundation and attended events at the old DeMille Barn in Los Angeles and eventually wrote two books about him.

   Once I got well underway with the process of writing this book, I went even deeper into the water of the word. Having completed Christine Kloser's *Transformational Author Experience,* I was already teaching creative writing classes at two different colleges. I went back through all of my old textbooks, including Anne Lamott's classic *Bird by Bird* and Robert McKee's *Story*. I wondered what I could really say that had not already been said by others in much better ways. I soon discovered that my own story needed to be told in a different way. When I was asked to write an article on Writing and Recovery for the *Recovery View* newsletter, I saw how my experience could benefit others in a unique way.

When you have been rooted into your story and called to fulfill your destiny, you will go through a baptism or immersion process in order to become initiated into the deepest levels of your subject. If that subject is your own life story, you are in for an even deeper adventure than you may have ever imagined.

5. **Crucifixion** – The seed falls to the ground and dies from its old existence. Moses and the children of Israel experienced the angel of death pass over them as the blood of the lamb saved them. A week after Jesus made his triumphal entry into Jerusalem to cheering crowds, he was turned over to the Roman authorities with a call from that same crowd

for his crucifixion. His last words were, "It is finished." Was that really the end of the story?

After I triumphantly finished what I thought was the final draft of *Transformed by Writing,* I submitted the manuscript for initial review to the executive editor at my publisher New Way Press. I waited eagerly for her response, expecting to hear songs of praises heralded by fanfare and showers of palm fronds. Instead I was told that my book wasn't worth the paper it was printed on – and this was a digital copy. In no uncertain terms, I was informed that my book would find its use in wiping the bottom of someone's shoes after a long walk through a dog park. Around the same time, I was told by one of my consultants that my intended title would subject me to scorn and ridicule and mark me forever as a phony, banning me forever from the gates of fame and fortune. I may be exaggerating a bit, but that's how I felt. What I was actually told was that the book needed some more revision and that I should consider a variation on my proposed title. Needless to say, I fell into a deep depression and shut myself away in my room pulling the covers over my head, never to awaken again. A few hours later, I got over it and went back to work.

When writing your book or screenplay, you will inevitably come to a point where all seems lost and you can't continue. The hero in your story will come to a place where there does not seem to be any way out. But you know that the seed that was originally planted and taken root will eventually spring forth unto new life.

6. **Resurrection** – The seed buried in the ground springs forth unto new life. The winter changes to spring. The great fish spewed forth Jonah from its belly and he continued his journey to Nineveh where preached his message and the entire city was saved. You can't have a resurrection without a crucifixion. Every story has a moment where all seems lost. If you've seen any of the *Indiana Jones* movies, you know it's where he's crossing over a rope bridge and the bad guys are chasing from behind with guns and spears and the bridge is on fire and there's no way he can possibly make it to the other side. One of my favorite scenes is in the *Temple of Doom* where Indiana Jones has to cross over a great chasm and actually has to step out onto an invisible bridge of faith.

   Moses led the children of Israel through the Red Sea when it miraculously parted and they escaped their former bondage in Egypt – once and for all. Jesus rose from the grave on the third day and defeated death. Neo in *The Matrix* died and rose again. The hero lives to tell the tale.

How does your story end? How does your character overcome impossible obstacles and achieve victory? When writing your book, keep the end in mind and look for ways to provide your reader with hope, healing, enlightenment, and inspiration.

I finished the book that you are holding in your hands in less than 90 days from when I began it. I know some of you are saying "wow" and others are saying, "Yeah, I can tell." Hey, go ahead and write your own book. The point is that I did it. So can you. Now get out there and do it. Tell your story.

7. **Transformation** – The final transformation is the changing of the caterpillar into the butterfly. The alchemist turns lead into gold. The seed has become a tree that now gives forth its fruit. The writer becomes a published author. Your movie shines on the big screen. The hero returns home to the praises of his people, shining with divine light and passing on the magic elixir of eternal life.

   How will writing change your life? How will you change the lives of others with your writing? How will you change the world?

Final Words

"You are the light of the world. A town built on a hill cannot be hidden. Neither do people light a lamp and put it under a bowl. Instead they put it on its stand, and it gives light to everyone in the house. In the same way, let your light shine before others, that they may see your good deeds and glorify your Father in heaven."

~ Jesus of Nazareth

Press Release Examples

Career Development Expert Reveals Success Secrets

Have you ever thought about writing a book, starting a business, getting in shape, or cleaning out your clutter, but you just don't have the time? With this technique it can happen.

FOR IMMEDIATE RELEASE

(Free-Press-Release.com) December 26, 2012 --
CONTACT: Info@newwaypress.com

Have you ever thought about writing a book, starting a business, getting in shape, or cleaning out your clutter, but felt like you just didn't have the time?

Lesa Hammond, PhD, career development expert and author of the Thompson Twins children's book series, has just released a new book designed to help people of all ages achieve their dreams in just 5 minutes a day. Achieve in 5! Transform Your Life in 5 Minutes a Day was written for individuals who think that they do not have time to accomplish their goals.

According to Hammond, “Many smart people with good ideas don't achieve their goals. It is not because they don't know how, but because they don't take the goal to the finish line.” Through a series of exercises, readings, and a daily practice of committing five minutes a day, readers develop a habit of success. Using the metaphor of a runner, Achieve in 5! provides a simple strategy to chart the course, mark the milestones, jump the hurdles, accept and follow helpful detours, and cross that finish line in just five minutes a day.

Hammond has worked with adults in transition for more than twenty years as a life coach, management consultant, and executive trainer. She is the Executive Director of Achievement U, a non-profit organization devoted to empowering young people to achieve their dreams. Hammond has appeared on numerous radio talk shows and has been interviewed for several articles in Black Enterprise magazine as an expert in career development and life transition.

Achieve in 5! Transform your Life in 5 Minutes a Day is available at amazon.com or Achieve in 5!

###

Achieve in 5!
Lesa Hammond
http://www.achievein5.com

Capital One Partners With Leading Author Robert Hammond to Educate Americans On Combating the Fastest Growing Crime in America

Exponential Rise in Identity Theft Indicates Need for Education

MCLEAN, Va., Sep 24, 2003 /PRNewswire-FirstCall via COMTEX/ -- Twenty-seven million Americans have been victims of identity theft in the last five years, according to the Federal Trade Commission. While identity theft could be anything from a hacker breaking into your online checking account to a thief using a stolen check, it is most often reported as credit card fraud (forty- two percent of incidents). To help combat this growing problem, leading credit card provider Capital One and noted author Robert Hammond, author of the book, Identity Theft, How to Protect Your Most Valuable Asset have joined forces to increase awareness and inform Americans on how to prevent identity theft and what to do if they do become a victim.

"While credit cards offer a great deal of convenience to consumers, it is important to realize what can happen if they fall into the wrong hands. Capital One helps by guaranteeing 100% fraud protection on any charges that are not made by the card holder," said Diana Don, Director of Financial Education at Capital One. "With the increase in identity theft, it is crucial to arm consumers with the knowledge to prevent fraud, and the tools to recover if they do become a victim."

"Most Americans don't believe they could become a victim of identity theft," said Hammond. "But what they don't know is that a growing number of identity theft crimes are committed by friends or family members. We're working to educate Americans on the realities of this crime, and provide them with simple tips to reduce their risk of becoming a victim."

Avoiding Identity Theft

Both Hammond and Don assert that one of the keys to

preventing identity theft is awareness, and encourage individuals to pay attention to their billing cycles and contact their creditors if bills do not arrive on time. Additionally, credit card users should know that identity theft is not committed just by anonymous hackers from a far away computer. In fact, according to the Federal Trade Commission, approximately 15% of individuals who reported identity theft were victimized by someone they knew: five percent of individuals were impacted by family members; two percent by friends or neighbors; one percent by an associate from work and five percent were known to the victim in some other capacity totaling 24,272 consumers.

"People should always be protective of personal information," said Hammond. "Never leave credit cards, credit card bills or solicitations lying around -- keep them in a safe place, or better yet, shred them."

Also, Hammond implores individuals to be extremely careful when selecting pin numbers. He strongly advises against using personal information that people know such as your birthday or street address. Also, for added security, delete your social security number from your driver's license.

"Consumers should never write down their passwords or carry them in a wallet or post them under a computer keyboard," says Hammond, "as criminals know where to look for it."

"Combating identity theft has been a passion of mine for years," said Robert Hammond. "I am proud to work with Capital One and lead the charge to educate consumers about this devastating crime."

If You Become a Victim
Report Back. Contact your creditors to close any fraudulent accounts that were opened in your name and notify all three national credit reporting agencies: Equifax, Experian and Trans Union.

Review and React. Obtain copies of your credit reports and ensure that no additional accounts have been opened in your name and follow-up with the fraud departments at the credit bureaus by sending them the disputed amounts in writing. Ensure that you order a new copy of your credit report every six months to verify that no fraudulent accounts have been opened in your name.

Keep Details. It is extremely important to keep records of your correspondence with the creditors, the credit bureaus as well as the local police. You never know when you may be called upon to provide evidence. Capital One offers an "Identity Theft Fraud Action Tracking Sheet", www.capitalone.com/credit101/fraud/FraudActionForm.doc to help track actions taken to handle the situation.

About Capital One

Headquartered in McLean, Virginia, Capital One Financial Corporation (NYSE: COF) (http://www.capitalone.com/) is a holding company whose principal subsidiaries include: Capital One Bank and Capital One, F.S.B., which offer consumer lending products, and Capital One Auto Finance, Inc., which offers auto loan products. Capital One's subsidiaries collectively had 45.8 million managed accounts and $60.7 billion in managed loans outstanding as of June 30, 2003. Capital One, a Fortune 500 company, is one of the largest providers of MasterCard and Visa credit cards in the world. Capital One trades on the New York Stock Exchange under the symbol "COF" and is included in the S&P 500 index.

SOURCE: Capital One Financial Corporation

Diana Don of Capital One, +1-703-720-2371, or
diana.don@capitalone.com, or
Jennifer Butler of MS&L, +1-212-468-3392, or
jennifer.butler@mslpr.com, for Capital One
http://www.capitalone.com

Bestselling Author Robert Hammond Releases the Light

Source: New Way Press Dated: Apr. 17, 2013

Mystical odyssey blends fantasy and true crime with visionary fiction, offering a ray of hope, inspiration, and recovery from addiction

WALNUT CREEK, Calif. -- *Have you seen the Light? He closed his eyes so nobody could see him.* The latest novel by bestselling author Robert Hammond, ***The Light*** (paperback, 978-0615796567) follows Abel Adams, a brilliant but troubled young misfit desperately seeking freedom, love, and spiritual enlightenment while battling drug addiction, dark forces, and strange temptations. Abel zigzags through a mysterious labyrinth of crime and the occult along his hazardous search for identity and self-realization.

The Light is the mystical odyssey of a prodigal son whose spiritual journey tumbles like a rollercoaster through philosophical, psychological, and religious experiences amid the turbulent post-1960s counterculture. Imagine a literary blend of *A Million Little Pieces* and *The Shack* with a twist.

Donna Kennedy of the Riverside Press-Enterprise compares the story to Joseph Conrad's *Heart of Darkness* when she says, "He entered the heart of darkness when his path branched into a labyrinth. Instead of 'the howl and the dance' of the African jungle that claimed Mr. Kurtz, [Abel Adams] was seduced by the world of hallucinogenic drugs. There is a new wisdom to author Hammond's quest for knowledge. Life is mystical."

Hammond calls *The Light* "a surrealistic adventure tale about transformation, spiritual enlightenment, and second chances." Facing rumors that the book's protagonist is a thinly-veiled alter ego of himself, Hammond says, "Abel Adams is essentially an allegorical composite of all of us who have gone astray at some point in our lives," says the author. "I believe that many people will discover they deeply identify with Abel's desperate desire for deliverance."

Watch video trailer here:
http://www.youtube.com/watch?v=OgkJ1rAD9zw
Hammond earned an MFA in Creative Writing and is an award-winning screenwriter, producer and author of over a dozen books, including *Ready When You Are: Cecil B. DeMille's Ten Commandments for Success* and *Blockbuster Resumes: Insider Secrets to Dazzle Your Audience and Blow Away the Competition.* In addition to developing projects for film and television, Hammond teaches screenwriting and is a popular speaker and talk-show guest on personal achievement, creativity, and spirituality. He has provided consulting to thousands of individuals, private organizations, and governmental agencies and was instrumental in establishing Riverside County's (CA) alternative dispute resolution and welfare-to-work programs.

The Light is available at www.NewWayPress.com and fine retailers everywhere.

--- End ---

Hollywood Producer Reveals Insider Secrets for Blockbuster Resumes

Source: New Way Press Dated: May 11, 2013

Award-winning writer-producer Robert Hammond helps job seekers dazzle their audience and blow away the competition.

LOS ANGELES, Calif. -- With national unemployment rates still at record levels, millions of Americans are wondering whether to keep looking or drop out of the labor market altogether. Others are stuck in dead-end or low-paying jobs and looking for a career change. Are you one of the many people who are struggling and sending out resumes, wondering why nobody is offering you a chance to prove your skills? What if a new kind of resume could help you land your next job interview?

Bestselling author and Hollywood producer Robert Hammond's new book *Blockbuster Resumes* (paperback, ISBN-13: 978-0615799254) combines his unique experience as a screenwriter and film industry creative executive with his decade-long background in government human resources consulting, management, and job development to provide job seekers with an easy-to-follow strategy to dazzle their audience and blow away the competition. *Blockbuster Resumes* also highlights the hottest new career trends and provides creative tools, templates, forms, and sample resumes that get proven results.

Blockbuster Resume book trailer:

http://www.youtube.com/watch?v=17QfaULh1ng

Hammond was instrumental in establishing Riverside County (CA)'s alternative dispute resolution and welfare-to-work programs. He also worked with the leadership of the California State Employment Development Department (EDD)'s Career One Stops and Workforce Investment Act (WIA) partners to develop online job training programs. He says, "Like Cecil B. DeMille's blockbuster movies,

Blockbuster Resumes are uniquely designed to dazzle your audience and blow away the competition."

Hammond says, "Blockbuster Resumes are perfect for newly graduating college students, military veterans, and people with long employment gaps as well as for high-level professionals wanting to totally change careers." Blockbuster Resumes are especially popular with actors, entertainment professionals, authors, academics, and executives looking for a one-page executive summary, LinkedIn profile, or bio. Certified Executive Coach Kristin Tomczak says, "This is where your Blockbuster Resume comes in...The average 'resume writer' wouldn't have a clue how to present, especially on one page, the greatness of individuals who've played big games, contributed big-time and want to do even more."

Hammond holds an MFA in Creative Writing and is an award-winning screenwriter and producer of the forthcoming *Cecil B. DeMille* biopic titled, *Hollywood.* He is the author of over a dozen books, including *C.B. DeMille: The Man Who Invented Hollywood, Ready When You Are: Cecil B. DeMille's Ten Commandments for Success*, and his latest novel, *The Light.*

Hammond is also a professor of creative writing and a popular speaker and talk-show guest on personal achievement, creativity, and Hollywood history.

Hammond created the website www.BlockbusterResume.org to provide free resume resources to job seekers and career counselors. His book, *Blockbuster Resumes: Insider Secrets to Dazzle Your Audience and Blow Away the Competition* is available at www.NewWayPress.com and fine retailers everywhere.

Ready When You Are: Cecil B. DeMille's Ten Commandments for Success

Source: New Way Press Dated: Jul. 29, 2012

What if the legendary director who invented Hollywood and the Biblical epic offered you his personal secrets to unlimited wealth and achievement?

The newly-released book, Ready When You Are: Cecil B. DeMille's Ten Commandments for Success (New Way Press) by Robert Hammond weaves the timeless wisdom of one of the greatest showman on earth into a detailed roadmap for successful living today.

Cecil B. DeMille is famous for such epics as The Ten Commandments, Cleopatra, and the Greatest Show on Earth and was one of the founders of early Hollywood and Paramount Pictures with seventy feature films to his credit.

Acclaimed filmmaker Steven Spielberg credits DeMille for inspiring him to make movies and "dream for a living." Spielberg says, "C.B. DeMille showed me how to put a lot of money up on the big screen and then make the studios pay for it."

DeMille's granddaughter, Cecilia de Mille Presley said that she considers Spielberg "the DeMille of today. Like Grandfather, he has consistently been able to capture vast audiences. He has had great commercial success without losing his personal vision or compromising his integrity."

In his latest book, comparable to such classics as The 7 Habits of Highly-Effective People, Think and Grow Rich, and Leadership Secrets of Attila the Hun, author Robert Hammond reveals C.B. DeMille's secret strategies to achieve a life of career success and personal fulfillment. In addition to being an inspirational self-help book, Ready When You Are also includes scholarly research on the influence of Cecil B. DeMille's Biblical epics as well as recently-discovered articles on filmmaking written by DeMille himself.

Hammond says, "I discovered these principles while working on my Master of Fine Arts in Creative Writing and researching the life of DeMille and the beginnings of the motion picture industry."

Robert Hammond is an award-winning screenwriter, author, and producer whose projects include the documentary One Day on Earth and the epic biopic C.B. DeMille: The Man Who Invented Hollywood. Hammond's previous books include Life After Debt, Credit Secrets, and Identity Theft. He has appeared on over 300 radio and television shows and is a highly sought-after speaker on screenwriting, filmmaking and Hollywood history.

Ready When You Are is now available in paperback and Kindle version at Amazon.com and fine bookstores everywhere.

New Novel Gives Cecil B. DeMille His Close-Up on Paramount Pictures' 100th Anniversary

Best-selling author Robert Hammond celebrates Paramount Pictures' 100th Anniversary with the release of his latest novel, "C.B. DeMille: The Man Who Invented Hollywood."

Los Angeles, CA - It seems that everyone in Hollywood is either talking about Paramount's 100th anniversary or giving out another award bearing the name of legendary director Cecil B. DeMille. Well get ready for the close-up because award-winning author and screenwriter Robert Hammond just released his latest novel entitled "C. B. DeMille: The Man Who Invented Hollywood." In this novelization of the beginnings of director Cecil B. DeMille's film career starting as a failed stage actor in the early 1900's, Hammond reveals the director's early family life in New York City, his relationship with his wife and young daughter and exposes his evident character flaws. In "C. B. DeMille: The Man Who Invented Hollywood," the reader will discover the origins of the then burgeoning film industry and what led DeMille to leave New York for a little-known southern California town called Hollywood, to follow his new calling as a film director.

Once out west, DeMille, along with Adolph Zukor and Jesse L. Lasky, form 'Famous Players-Lasky Corporation' later changed to 'Paramount Famous Lasky Corporation' the forerunner to Paramount Pictures Studios. Hammond's lightning-paced novel highlights the great filmmaker's Hollywood odyssey of excess, infidelity, redemption and reverence, leading to the most celebrated figure in entertainment history and the "Greatest Showman on Earth." Hammond's previous book, "Ready When You Are: Cecil B. DeMille's Ten Commandments for Success" (New Way Press) was also released last month.

"C. B. DeMille" is already making waves in Hollywood and an adaptation is in development as an epic biopic. Cecil B. DeMille is getting ready for his own close-up.

Hollywood Producer Receives Governor's Pardon

California Governor Jerry Brown pardons award-winning writer-producer and author Robert Hammond

SACRAMENTO, CA — Gov. Edmund G. Brown Jr. pardoned 65 convicted felons on the eve of Easter, including noted author and Hollywood producer Robert Hammond. Stating in a news release that they had "demonstrated exemplary behavior following their conviction(s)," the pardons restore their citizenship, including the right to serve on a jury.

Hammond was sentenced in Riverside County Superior Court Oct. 30, 1997 for selling or furnishing a controlled substance and possession of a firearm. He served 11 months in prison and a year of parole before being discharged on Christmas Day in 1999.

After spending more than half his life in and out of jails, rehabs, and prisons while battling drug addiction, Hammond earned an MFA in Creative Writing and became an award-winning screenwriter, producer known for such films as *Destiny's Lance*, *The Green Bandits*, and the forthcoming *Cecil B. DeMille* biopic titled, *Hollywood.* He is the author of over a dozen books, including *C.B. DeMille: The Man Who Invented Hollywood* and *Ready When You Are: Cecil B. DeMille's Ten Commandments for Success*. As the author of *Identity Theft: How to Protect Your Most Valuable Asset,* Hammond was the spokesperson for Capital One Financial Corporation's Identity Theft Prevention Program.

In addition to developing projects for film and television, Hammond is a professor of creative writing and a popular speaker and talk-show guest on personal achievement, creativity, and Hollywood history. He has provided consulting to thousands of individuals, private organizations, and governmental agencies and was instrumental in establishing Riverside County's (CA) alternative dispute resolution and welfare-to-work programs.

He recently worked with the leadership of the California State Employment Development Department (EDD)'s Career One Stops and Workforce Investment Act (WIA) partners to create a training program based on his book *Blockbuster Resumes: Insider Secrets to Dazzling Your Audience and Blowing Away the Competition.*

Hammond just released his semi-autobiographical novel, *The Light* (New Way Press, 978-0615796567), a mystical odyssey that follows Abel Adams, a brilliant but troubled young misfit desperately seeking freedom, love, and spiritual enlightenment while battling drug addiction, dark forces, and strange temptations. He calls *The Light* "a surrealistic adventure tale about transformation, spiritual enlightenment, and second chances." Admitting that the book's protagonist is a thinly-veiled alter ego of himself, Hammond says, "Abel Adams is essentially an allegorical composite of all of us who have gone astray at some point in our lives," says the author. "I believe that many people will discover they deeply identify with Abel's desperate desire for deliverance." The film adaptation of *The Light* is in the works.

Book Excerpt

Finding the Light Within

By the time you read this, I'll be gone.

I woke up blindfolded and tied to a chair. A distant voice whispered, "Have you seen the light?" I shook and struggled desperately to loosen myself from my bonds.

So begins my novel, *The Light,* a mystical odyssey about spiritual enlightenment and second chances.

Have you seen the Light?

Who is the one that does the seeing?

How can you find that which is within you and all around you?

What is the sound of one hand slapping your face before your grandfather was born in the forest with nobody around to hear it?

As a long-time spiritual truth-seeker, I have studied many books, attended many meetings, and practiced many disciplines. I have written books, produced films, taught college, and provided consulting services to thousands of individuals, business organizations, and governmental agencies on a variety of subjects. I've also had my share of troubles and misadventures along the way, including some dangerous detours and deceptions.

Like many people, I've struggled with emotional, financial, health and relationship issues. I've sought solutions through so many sources I would not have time to list them all. For many years, I walked in the darkness of deception and despair, thinking I could see when I was truly blind. Finally, in the deepest depths of darkness of death's doorstep I found the Light.

After many years of arduous seeking and stumbling, I discovered a path to personal freedom, happiness, and spiritual enlightenment that was so simple and yet so profound that you may wonder why it took so long to be revealed. What if the answers you've been looking for have been hiding in plain sight all along?

Among my most profound realizations was that what I had been seeking was within me and all around me all along. With so many divisions, distractions and deceptions in the world, finding the Light is not as easy as it seems. But if you seek it you will find it.

Finding the Light Within: A Spiritual Guide to True Peace, Happiness, Freedom, and Enlightenment offers:

- Three steps to spiritual enlightenment.
- A new way of looking at the world that will change your life forever.
- Simple and practical ways to overcome negativity emotions and destructive behavior.
- Inspiration and hope that you will want to share with your friends and loved ones.

Finding the Light Within: A Spiritual Guide to True Peace, Happiness, Freedom, and Enlightenment reveals some of the most startling and unique insights on the process of finding the inner light ever revealed. You will discover the transformational writings of 17th century mystics George Fox, Stephen Crisp, Madame Jeanne Guyon, Francois Fenelon, and Miguel de Molinos that were once banned by governments and religious authorities.

A word of caution: your preconceptions are about to be shattered and your perception of reality altered forever. What you are about to read will transform your mind and heart to a completely new level of experience and understanding. I encourage you to share this book with others. May the eyes of your understanding be enlightened.

Everyone is enlightened. The light is within you and all around you. Be still and know.

Recommended Resources

Books

Hammond, Lesa, *Achieve in 5! Transform Your Life in Just 5 Minutes a Day,* New Way Press, 2012.

Hammond, Robert, et al., *Finding the Light Within: The Spiritual Guide to True Peace, Happiness, Freedom, and Enlightenment,* New Way Press, 2013.

Hammond, Robert, *The Light, a novel,* New Way Press, 2012.

Hammond, Robert, *Blockbuster Resumes: Insider Secrets to Dazzle Your Audience and Blow Away the Competition,* New Way Press. 2012.

Hammond, Robert, *C.B. DeMille: The Man Who Invented Hollywood,* New Way Press, 2012.

Hammond, Robert, *Ready When You Are: Cecil B. DeMille's Ten Commandments for Success,* New Way Press. 2011.

Other Resources

New Way Press –independent, collaborative publishers of books that change lives www.NewWayPress.com

Robert Hammond Consulting

Writing and Consulting Services

Do you want to write a book or screenplay and need help? www.roberthammondconsulting.com

Consulting services include:

- Analysis (Concept, Market, Platform, Story)
- Author Bios
- Book Proposals
- Brainstorming
- Career Coaching
- Concept Development
- Creative Consulting
- Film and Television Adaptation
- Ghost Writing
- Loglines and Taglines
- Marketing and Technical Research
- Referrals and Other Resources
- Unlocking Your Creative Flow
- Zeroing in on Your Personal Story and Purpose

For a free initial consultation, contact:
Robert@RobertHammondConsulting.com

Achieve in 5! Learn how to transform your life and achieve your dreams in just 5 minutes a day. Consulting services, classes, and publications.
www.achievein5.com

C.B. DeMille – The movie. Find out more about the epic biopic featuring the man who gave Hollywood its close-up. www.cbdemille.com

Blockbuster Resumes - Ready to brand yourself and build a blockbuster bio?
Visit: www.blockbusterresume.org

A Film Writer - Terri Zinner's Screenwriting Coverage, Classes, and Related Services. www.afilmwriter.com

Voyage Media - Nat Mundel's group provides classes and services related to adapting books to screenplays as well as film and television development, including look books and packaging. www.voyagemedia.com

Internet Transcribers - Paul Klein and his company do an excellent job with transcribing mp3 audios such as teleseminars, radio interviews, and even YouTube videos to word docs. This is a great way to turn your talking into writing and get your book done. www.InternetTranscribers.com

Transformational Author Experience - Christine Kloser's comprehensive online training program was a catalyst for getting me to write this book. Excellent resources for aspiring authors.

www.transformationalauthor.com

Bostick Communications – Low cost press release distribution to media outlets.
www.bostickcommunications.com

Main Street Media Savvy. Nancy Juetten, author of the Bye Bye Boring Bio is an expert on bios and media promotion.
www.mainstreetmediasavvy.com

Radio and Television Interview Report (RTIR). Steve Harrison's bi-monthly advertising and copywriting service for authors and radio and talk show guests. www.rtir.com

Reader Views – Publicity, book reviews and related services for self-published authors.
www.readerviews.com

About the Author

ROBERT HAMMOND is an award-winning screenwriter, producer and author of over a dozen books including *The Light* and *Ready When You Are: Cecil B. DeMille's Ten Commandments for Success*. In addition to developing projects for film and television, Hammond is a literary consultant and a popular talk-show guest on personal transformation, creativity, and Hollywood history.

Hammond has appeared on over 300 radio and television programs. As the author of *Identity Theft: How to Protect Your Most Valuable Asset,* Hammond was the spokesperson for Capital One Financial Corporation's Identity Theft Prevention Program.

He holds a Master of Fine Arts degree in Creative Writing and teaches screenwriting. His mission is to help others find their inner light and share their stories with the world.

For more information visit:
RobertHammondConsulting.com

www.ingramcontent.com/pod-product-compliance
Lightning Source LLC
LaVergne TN
LVHW091053080826
845145LV00002B/734

9780615875958